BORN *to be*

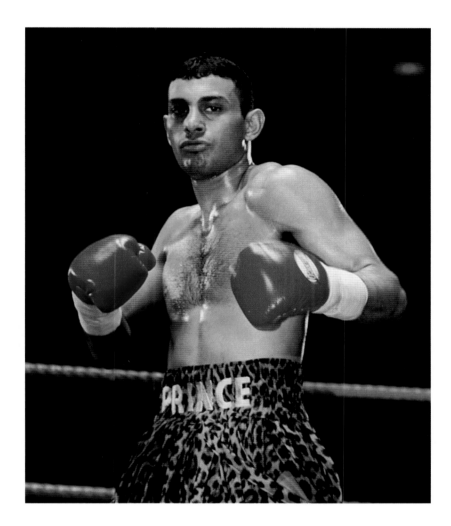

KING

BORN
TO BE
KING

The Rise of
PRINCE NASEEM HAMED

Ian Stafford

CONTENTS

Round One
The King is Dead,
Long Live the King 6

Round Two
A Prince's Palace 18

Round Three
The Sorcerer's Apprentice 28

Round Four
The Prince Earns His Spurs 36

Round Five
Big Time 46

Round Six
Defence of the Realm 54

Round Seven
A Star is Born 72

Round Eight
On Top of the World 82

Fight card 94

The tale of the tape 95

The king is dead, *long live the* KING

The king is dead,
long live the king:
Frank Bruno crowns
the young pretender.

Thirty-five seconds! Or, to put it another way, four punches. The equation was simplicity itself. Three punches equalled three knockdowns and a stagger, making the Alamo look like an even contest in comparison. The crowd did not quite know whether to cheer for their hero, or jeer as they tried to work out just what they got for their £100-plus ringside seats.

Welcome to the world of 'Prince' Naseem Hamed, and another ritual slaughter carried out by the fastest, most charismatic, most precocious and, if you listen to anyone in the know, most talented young British fighter seen this side of the Second World War. You can be guaranteed to witness a spectacular fight when this character is involved but be warned – blink, and you may miss the action. Opposing boxers may as well heed the same advice. Blink, and you may be staring up at

the ceiling from the canvas.

The month of March and, in particular, the night of March 16th, 1996, will prove to be a significant date in British boxing. Considering the fact that Hamed had taken his first world title, the WBO World Featherweight championship, after demolishing Steve Robinson in his previous fight, it may seem a little strange to highlight what turned out to be a routine, first defence for a young man just turned 22 years old. But it was the way he conducted his business that night, coupled with events elsewhere, that reinforced what Hamed had always told anyone who cared to listen – he had been born to be king, and that night he acquired the throne.

A fortnight earlier the boxing promoter and entrepreneur, Frank Warren, had enjoyed the luxury of three world champions, and the

biggest names in British boxing to boot, in his Hertford-based, Sports Network stable. 'Prince' Naseem Hamed, or 'Naz' to virtually everyone who knows him, may have been the most exciting of the triumvirate, but was nevertheless the most junior member of this rather exclusive club. He knew that time was on his side, and was momentarily prepared to share the limelight with Nigel Benn and Frank Bruno.

And so it finally showed, on March 2nd, when Benn was comprehensively beaten by the unfancied South African, Sugar Boy Malinga. His night ended in tears, an announcement that he had retired, and a marriage proposal to his long-suffering partner – since then the retirement part has been shelved.

One down, but still two remaining. For once, Hamed was quite happy to be the hors

Frank Bruno and Naz sign for Sky TV. Promoter Frank Warren makes the announcement at a packed press conference.

The other two were both in the twilight of their careers. For Benn, the WBC Super-Middleweight champion, it was just a question of when, and how, he would quit. Any self-respecting boxer will tell you that even the best in the ring can only live through a small number of epic encounters. Nigel Benn had somehow contrived to have been involved in some of the very best fights seen in British rings in recent years. His two controversial clashes with Chris Eubank and, in particular, his miraculous recovery against the ultimately tragic American, Gerald McClellan, were bound to pay a heavy toll.

d'oeuvres two weeks later. Even he conceded that his first title defence, at the Scottish Exhibition Centre in Glasgow, paled into insignificance compared to the big meeting in Las Vegas later that same night – Bruno versus Tyson II, only this time it was Bruno who held the WBC World Heavyweight champion's belt, and Tyson the hungry challenger.

Of course, we all hoped big Frank would surprise the pundits in his first world title defence and defeat a man who, so many believed, was bound to have lost his edge and stomach for a major fight in the previous three years' serving his time in an Indianapolis prison after his conviction for rape. Instead, Tyson appeared stronger and more determined than ever, punishing a seemingly frozen Bruno from the first bell, until the comforting arms of the referee ended proceedings midway through the third round.

And then there was one. A few hours earlier, late into the Saturday night, Naz had swatted his Nigerian challenger, Said Lawal, with contemptuous ease. By dawn on Sunday, Hamed was Britain's only, high-profile world champion.

The first time I actually came across this little boxing phenomenon from Sheffield was back in the late 1980s, when I used to visit the Wincobank gymnasium where the trainer, Brendan Ingle, presides with a fatherly eye over his young charges. All attention was then focused on boxers Herol 'Bomber' Graham and Johnny Nelson, and not a cocky little youngster who, unbeknown to us at the time, would take to the big time like a well-cut suit.

It was in April 1992, when I first saw Hamed in action, appearing as very much a side-show, at Manchester's G-Mex Centre, on the undercard of a Chris Eubank World Super Middleweight title defence against an American called John Jarvis.

Ingle, now 54 years old, had been muttering the boy's name to me for a couple of years beforehand, but he had not prepared me for what took place that night. While Eubank dismissed his opponent with a powerful right hook in the third round, it was a skinny Hamed, just five foot three inches in height, who stuck in my mind.

Most boxers, of course, make an impact inside the ring. Everyone who follows sport now knows all about Hamed's over-the-top entrances but, back then, nobody had heard of him, which made his approach to the ropes even more memorable. While James Brown blasted out 'I Feel Good' over the tannoy system, a lean, young Arab boy, clad in his now token leopard skin shorts,

danced his way to the ring.

Normally, unless you are a member of the family, a friend, an associate within the sport or a total boxing afficionado, you pay

little attention to the fighters who first appear on a world title undercard, and absolutely no interest in the mere entrance of a youngster set to make just his second professional appearance.

Naseem Hamed defied you to look

Naz spots the cameras after demolishing Said Lawal in Glasgow, flanked by his delighted father, Sal, and trainer Brendan Ingle.

anywhere else but at him. So, as 'The
Godfather of Soul' yelled 'So Good' Hamed
pointed both his gloves towards
himself, stopping abruptly from his shimmies
between the rows and rows of seats, before
gyrating his body again while Brown
reminded us that he really did feel good.

You could hear it all around you: 'Just
who is this kid?' And you could see it all
around the auditorium. Expressions changed
from bemusement to amusement. The great
irony of the night was that Hamed upstaged
the so-called great entertainer's entrance.
Chris Eubank was supposed to be the man
who had everybody watching him as he
made his rather superior way to the ringside.
With his flared nostrils, his gentle touching
of gloves, a long stare at the crowd, a two-

footed vault over the ropes and a couple of
extra poses, all to the thumping music of
Tina Turner's 'Simply the Best', Eubank was
the act guaranteed to put bums on seats. In
his case, it helped to disguise some of his
lack-lustre displays that were becoming
increasingly questioned.

In Hamed's case, the entrance, which he
claims Eubank tried to pinch after studying
the young Arab performing backflips and
somersaults during training, was just the
beginning. I was there to report on Eubank,
so the last thing I expected was to be riveted
to my seat watching a seemingly unimportant
and irrelevant fight on the undercard. All
around me, people were sharing the
experience. Did that Arab boy really just
perform a back somersault in the ring during

a round? Has his opponent managed to lay even one glove on him yet? Did you see the punch that ended the fight in the second round because, together with the hapless Shaun Norman inside the ropes, I'm damned if I did?

Over the next couple of years Hamed's reputation grew as quickly as his impressive record. Each fighter went more or less the same way, succumbing to someone, and something, they had never experienced before in the sport. Mesmerized and bewildered, they all returned to their homes none the wiser for what had befallen them.

V for Victory, and with his damaged hand. A message from Naz to those who doubted him after he injured his hand in training. Said Lawal has lasted just four punches.

11

Come on, get up! Naz wants more, but Enrique Angeles has other ideas.

I recall speaking to the manager of the Italian, Antonio Picardi, who failed dismally to take away Hamed's newly-won European title in August 1994. It was an hour after Hamed had teased, tortured and finally tossed away his opponent inside nine minutes, and Picardi was supposed to be the official number one challenger. 'Is it right that Hamed was dancing in his dressing-room before the fight?' the manager asked. I confirmed this to be true, and watched as he shuffled away, shaking his head in disbelief. I didn't have the heart to tell him that Hamed had also been playing pool with his mates, watching 'Beavis and Butthead' on television, chanting out the lyrics to his favourite 'jungle music' and chatting away to me.

Under two years later that same Arab kid was on course to deliver everything he had promised. Said Lawal represented opponent number 21 in the professional ranks for Hamed, and if his Nigerian counterpart had studied the 'Prince's' record, he might have been forgiven for placing a large bet on the other guy. Twenty previous fights had all ended in the same, unforgiving way, with eighteen members of the opposition failing to even get close to the last round. Two boxers had the temerity to only lose on points, but since May 1994, Hamed had always preferred to finish his night's work early.

The record clearly was impressive, but that was only half of it. It is only when you study Hamed's individual attributes that

The usual low-key entrance from Naz, this time at Michael Watson's benefit show at the Grosvenor House hotel.

Just another night's work: Naz beats Freddy Cruz to take the WBC International Super-Bantamweight championship. Brendan Ingle and Frank Warren stand to his right.

you come to the conclusion that, despite his tender age, he is already close to being the complete boxer.

Some fighters are known for the power of their punching, like our own Frank Bruno, while others are renowned for their hand speed, like Hamed's former colleague in Wincobank, Herol Graham, but few can boast an unbeatable combination of both.

Hamed has the ability to throw a total of 36 punches in just eight seconds, all of which are hard enough to make most opponents collapse into a crumpled heap. So hard are his punches that there have been occasions when he has hurt sparring partners three stones heavier than himself.

Okay then, what's his stamina like? Despite his record of quickly dispatching his

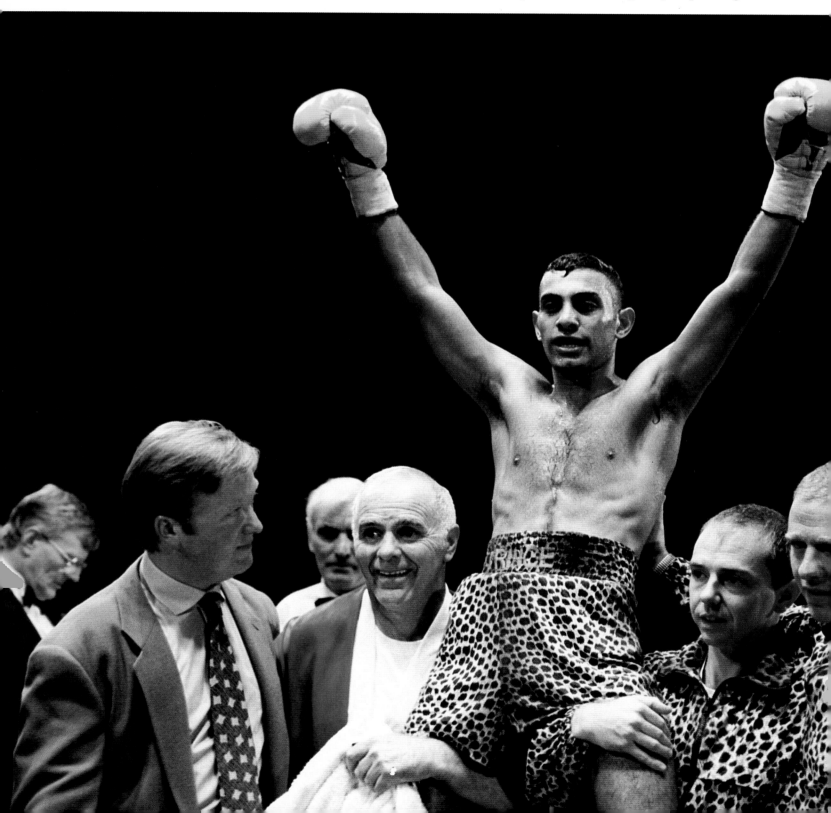

opponents he displayed, when relieving Italy's Vincenzo Belcastro of his European Bantamweight title in May 1994, colossal energy and work rate. Belcastro, an experienced and highly-respected fighter in his own right, found it impossible to wear Hamed down, and was demoralized to see his young pretender dancing at the final bell.

What about his balance? Again, ask Belcastro. The Italian could not land a decent punch in twelve, gruelling rounds, because Hamed ran, ducked and bounced back on his toes, perfectly distributing his weight to deliver numbing counter punches.

And so the list continues. Anticipation – he possesses a sixth sense which he puts to effective use by being the most aware boxer currently earning a living. As many who have fought him have since admitted, they could have sworn they had Hamed's head right where they wanted it to be, only to end up punching thin air. Agility – his somersaulting entrance into the ring may be designed to create interest in him, but it also carries a strong statement of intent to the man he is about to meet. Hamed's speed around the ring is universally recognized as breathtaking, ensuring that in the rare event that he faces potential danger, his legs whisk him away to safety. Chin – often the one soft spot that makes the difference between a champion and a contender of Marlon Brando's proportions. Steve Robinson landed the occasional punch on Hamed, punches that had helped him win and repeatedly defend his world title, but this time his young challenger just laughed in his face. Ring sense, spontaneity, ability to handle pressure, you name it, Naseem Hamed seems to possess it all.

Perhaps, though, there was a ray of hope for Said Lawal, that night back in March. Despite Hamed's credentials, one or two question marks had been raised about the young champion in the days running up to the clash. They stemmed from the postponement of Hamed's initially planned first defence against the Mexican, Arnulfo Castillo, which should have taken place at the London Arena the previous December. Hamed fractured his right hand in training and was forced to pull out.

Assuming that Hamed had to have a weakness, some talk in boxing circles wondered if he would recover his full punching power in the right hand, and whether such an injury was a bad portent for the future. The fact that Hamed predicted he

would knock Lawal out with a left hook only served to fuel suspicions that he would be protecting his damaged other hand. It had been six months since Hamed had last fought, winning the WBO title against Robinson in September 1995, and that made it the longest gap in between fights since the young man turned professional back in April

It was a great shot, the first shot hit him so hard that he had to go.

1992. In hindsight, the words 'clutching' and 'straws' come to mind, but prior to the fight some could argue that the omens were not entirely in Hamed's favour.

It was to the theme music of the film, 'The Omen', that Hamed made his spectacular entrance, ever-conscious of entertaining the viewers of Sky Sports, who had become his major paymasters. A firework display picked out his name in the corner of the stadium from where the fighters had emerged from the dressing-room. Hamed then proceeded to dance his way to the ringside, before performing his customary somersault over the ropes. The whole event took a full five minutes, which turned out to be considerably longer than the following bout.

The Austrian-based Lawal, the WBO's officially fourth-ranked featherweight, a man beaten just twice in a nineteen-fight career, and the WBC's International champion, refused to look at Hamed before the start of the fight, but still seemed overawed by the atmosphere, and by the razzmatazz of the world champion's entrance.

If Lawal was hoping to knuckle down to the fight, Hamed had other ideas. Springing from the corner at the sound of the first bell with a confident swagger, Hamed landed a straight right at lightning speed with his suspect right hand that not only sent Lawal crashing to the canvas in a heap, but also broke his nose. 'It was a great shot,' Naz concluded later. 'The first shot hit him so hard that he had to go.' The time on the clock read three seconds.

Rising to his feet after a count of five, but still obviously groggy, Lawal's legs trembled, while his body swayed. Many fights have been stopped at such a stage, but the Puerto Rican referee, Ismael Fernandez, perhaps mindful of the fight's ridiculously short duration, allowed the proceedings to continue.

The second punch, also, tellingly, a right, failed to produce quite such a withering effect, but was still strong enough to send Lawal staggering and stumbling on to the ropes, from where Hamed took a long and theatrical look at his opponent. 'He still thinks he's fighting later on tonight', was how he described Lawal later.

A third punch, a repeat dosage with the right, sent Lawal crashing down on to his knees, and almost before he was standing again the Nigerian found himself back on the canvas, courtesy of yet another right-hander from Hamed. Referee Fernandez had no other option but to call it a day, waving his hands in the air as the second hand on the clock ticked on to 35 seconds.

This is a record for a bout at such a level, beating by ten seconds Lloyd Honeyghan's welterweight defence against Gene Hatcher in 1989, although, in reality, Hamed had won the fight as soon as his first right-hander had found its target. Had the referee been as rigorous with his officiating as Hamed was merciless with his punches, the 22-year-old from Sheffield would have registered the fastest knockout in world championship history.

For a short while afterwards some of the

6,000 crowd at the Scottish Exhibition Centre threw their programmes into the ring and voiced their dissent as Lawal was led away in tears. The protests were not directed so much at Hamed, but because they felt they had been short-changed. At this rate, Naseem Hamed is becoming too superior for his own good.

The man in question was only bothered by one aspect of the fight afterwards. Any queries about his right hand had firmly been put in their place, and his world title remained safe in his possession, but Naseem Hamed still felt the need to apologize.

'I said I'd finish it in the second,' he said. 'But that first shot was too hard so, what the hell, I ended it a round early.' His predicting, normally spot on, may have been blemished, but his confidence remained blissfully intact. 'I'm going to beat all of them. I'm going to be a legend.'

On the night that boxing so cruelly exposed Frank Bruno, the Prince became a King, as his motto had always promised. 'I've said it all along, haven't I? Right from the very start.'

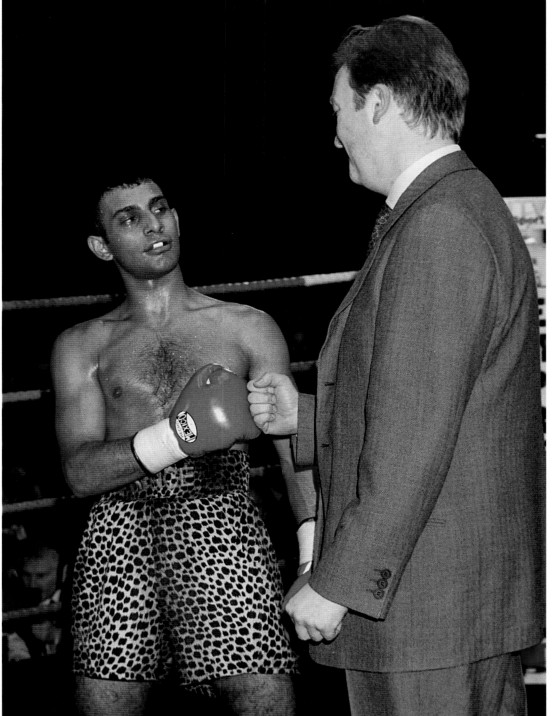

One week before he defends his newly-acquired WBC International Super-Bantamweight crown, in November 1994, Naz tells his promoter Frank Warren how it is.

A prince's
PALACE

Naz faces up to the unpredictable threat posed by a seven-year-old boy.

Notice the safety aspect nailed to the wall, which is so important to Brendan Ingle.

To this day Brendan Ingle cannot decide whether it was pure coincidence or fate taking a hand that brought him together with Naseem Hamed. Whatever the case, it makes the chorus girl turning into the star scenario seem commonplace in comparison. It is the kind of story that will be told so often that, in the true tradition of Chinese Whispers, the facts will no doubt soon change beyond all recognition. So let us record it now while it remains true to the original.

The Irish trainer recalls sitting on the top deck of a bus winding its way through the streets of Wincobank, one of the poorer suburbs of northern Sheffield, fifteen years ago. He happened to glance into a school-yard and saw a little, dark-skinned lad, whom he assumed to be of Pakistani origin, surrounded by three, clearly older kids, and fighting them off.

'He was dodging in and out and giving them what for,' Ingle tells you to this day, his voice excited and as thick as Irish buttermilk. 'He was ducking and punching beautifully. They couldn't land a shot on him. It struck me, even then, that he had natural movement and a knack of avoiding blows. It should have been no contest, because the other kids were twice his size, but even at that age he showed no fear.' Ingle rushed home and told his wife, Alma, what he had just seen.

A week later Salem Hamed brought three of his sons, Riath, Nabil and Naseem, to Ingle's gymnasium. 'I'm having trouble with my boys,' he told the trainer. 'They get picked on because they are Arabs.' Ingle looked at Naseem Hamed and instantly recognized the little kid in the playground. Naseem, in return, looked around the tatty gymnasium. This was to become his second home from that point onwards.

His parents, Salem and Caria, had come to Britain from the Yemen in the 1950s. Yemen included the former British colony of Aden, and during Sheffield's steel boom many Yemenis emigrated to the city to hold noisy, shopfloor jobs shunned by British employees. They were one of the first ethnic

families to move into the area and, within a couple of years, had earned enough money to start up a newsagent-cum-grocery business. Compared to many of their countrymen, the Hameds fared well. Since the decline of the

Naz has to try and avoid being hit while keeping his hands behind his back.

steel industry many Sheffield-based Yemenis have suffered poverty and high unemployment, made worse, of course, by race discrimination.

distinguish between Arabs and Asians. 'I was good at fighting in the streets because I needed to be', Hamed tells you. 'Kids attacked me because I was an Arab and had

No matter how hard the boy tries, he fails to land one punch on his slippery opponent. No wonder even world-class boxers find it difficult to touch Naz.

Naz was born in Sheffield on February 12th, 1974. In Arabic, 'Naseem' means 'gentle breeze'. As far as his opponents in the ring are concerned, the translation of the name 'Naseem' is closer to a 'hurricane'. One of a brood of five boys and four girls, his early childhood was spent in an area where racism was rife. He and his brothers can remember being repeatedly called 'Pakis' at school. The racial slurs were bad enough, but some of their fellow pupils were too ignorant to

a different colour of skin to the white or black kids.' By 1981, even though Naseem was just seven years old, their proud father felt that enough was enough. It was to Brendan Ingle, and his gym, that he turned.

Ingle was one of a family of fifteen before he moved from Dublin to Sheffield to mix boxing with working at the steelworks. He, and a local vicar, Fred Herrington, converted a battered school building into the St Thomas' Boys Club, which now stands opposite the church on Newnham Road. It is only half a mile away from the extravagance of the new Meadowhall shopping complex, but it may as well be on another planet, for these are some of the poorest, most underprivileged streets in Sheffield, if not in Britain.

The little boy's second home would have made even the most imaginative estate agent struggle to find anything good to say about it. Run down and musty, with paint peeling and sweat seemingly worked into the very fabric of the walls, you get no frills at St Thomas' Boys Club. Nothing much has changed in the intervening fifteen years.

During this time Brendan Ingle had been the nearly man. He had enjoyed some success, but had had to endure, from the agonies of the ringside corner, his charges fall at the final, and stiffest, hurdle. You will still see a life-size, cardboard cut out of Herol 'Bomber' Graham, for example, leaning against one of the walls in the gym.

For many, before Hamed came along, Graham seemed to have it all. He was the complete Ingle creation – slippery, quick on his feet, fast with his hands, and possessing a great defence. To this day many boxing pundits describe the Bomber as the best middleweight never to win a world title. The best in the business made sure that they never met Graham during his prime because they knew what was likely to befall them. Instead, notably against Mike McCallum, Graham failed by the narrowest of margins to become the world champion. The defeat against the hard-hitting Julian Jackson, when Graham was so far ahead that, momentarily, he let his guard drop, allowing the struggling American to drop him with a perfect hook, was particularly hard for Ingle to take.

'For years I'd been ridiculed by others in boxing for my methods', Ingle has since told me on various occasions. The sight of a distraught Graham on the canvas merely confirmed the views of many rival trainers and promoters in the game. When it comes to the big time, Ingle and his methods were

out of their depth.

It is therefore a delicious irony that Naseem Hamed, without doubt Ingle's greatest triumph, has become a total vindication of his methods laughed at by many in the cut-throat and back-stabbing world of the fight game. 'So many people have scoffed at what I've been trying to achieve because I've never done things by the book', Ingle says. 'I've always been a believer of fighters adopting an unorthodox style because an opponent never then quite knows what's coming. I made Naz watch people like Fred Astaire dancing and then copy it in the ring, because that can be so much more productive than hours of bag work or sparring. It's taken me thirty years to develop my ideal fighter, and now I have him.'

At a time when the morals and safety of boxing continue to remain under the microscope, Ingle can be forgiven for holding his head up high in pride. If you stick your neck around the door of the Wincobank gym you should be prepared for one of the strangest sights in British sport, let alone boxing. For even today, at an initial glance, it may seem that the biggest name in British boxing is beating up a succession of small boys inside an elevated boxer's training ring. But before you reach for the telephone and the number for the NSPCC, look a bit harder.

In reality, Naseem Hamed is not laying a glove on the eager eight-, nine- and ten-year-olds. Try as they might, the boys are hurling left hook after right hook, uppercut after jab at the slippery boxer. Each time the shots end up harmlessly in the air.

This is the secret of Brendan Ingle's gym. His unorthodox (some say crazy) methods are now paying dividends in a big way. The trainer may have enjoyed previous success with Herol Graham and Johnny Nelson, but it is Naseem Hamed who has convinced the highly traditional world of boxing that Ingle is not just another 'mad Irishman'.

While nearly every boxer I've ever known or seen slugs it out with a willing opponent in the ring during sparring, much of Hamed's

training has been carried out with kids so small that their large gloves look almost comical at the end of their wiry arms. Seeing this for the first time, I had to ask Naz a simple question – why?

don't really know all the moves in boxing. This means, unlike most adult boxers, they are unpredictable, and sling punches from all directions. The end result is that I'm prepared for anything in the ring.'

Brendan Ingle lends his advice to his young protégé during the Castro fight.

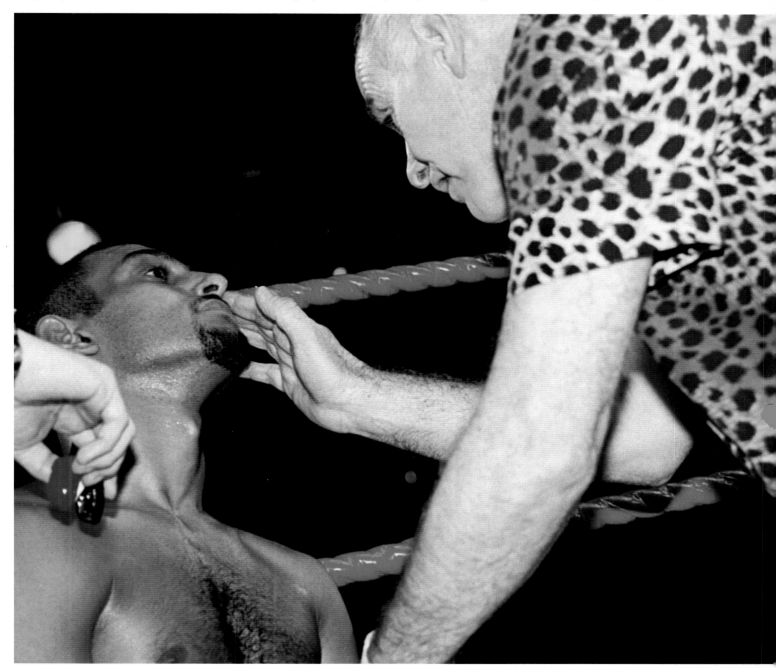

'I know it must look daft, but these kids give me the best training possible', he replied. 'For a start, they are so eager to hit me, which means I can't slacken for a moment. And because they are still so young, they

The method is pretty safe. Hamed is not allowed to hit back, instead he dances around the ring, at an incredible speed and turn of foot, with his hands behind his back. No wonder he is virtually impossible to catch.

(opposite) The Glasgow crowd are treated to a little gymnastics from their hero during his successful defence of his WBC International Super-Bantamweight title against Armando Castro.

Ingle's motives here are twofold. While deaths and tragic injuries continue to haunt the fight game, the genial Irishman has bent over backwards to ensure, first and foremost, the safety of his boxers. On the walls of the gym, in big capital letters, are notices reading: 'Boxing can damage your health', and 'Important – no sparring without supervision. For your own safety, gumshields and headguards must be worn'. All it lacks is an official Government health warning.

But there is another, tactical reason why Ingle is so cautious. 'Put it this way,' he explains. 'The best football teams don't concede many goals, do they?' Indeed, they do not. It is a method he has adopted in boxing ever since it first came to him, back in the 1970s.

'I was only a modest middleweight, but when I gave it up in 1974, it was Henry Cooper who gave me the idea. He used to win all his fights, then he started to lose. He was beaten because he always cut badly, and the reason why he was cut was because he kept on being hit.'

'Don't forget, boxing is the only sport where you can legally kill someone, so nobody should underestimate the danger. I certainly don't, which is why I train my boxers the way I do. If they're not hit, they can't lose. And if they're not hit, they can't be hurt. What more can any boxer want than that? Remember, in this game, your health is your wealth.'

Ever-conscious of the worst scenario in boxing, Hamed has the skill to choose his shots at will, ensuring both an emphatic, but safe result. 'I'm very aware of safety through this gym,' he says. 'This is why I've mastered the body shot. You can't be badly hurt there. I'm in the ring to box, not to kill someone or get killed. There have been times when I could have done a lot of damage and finished someone off, but the fight's over and I've done enough.'

There is one, final factor, behind Ingle's crusade. His modest house is directly opposite the gym, which means that he can be

Naz shows Vincenzo Belcastro a move which cannot be found in any text book on his way to claiming the European Bantamweight crown. Everything Naz is doing here, from his footwork to his hand movement, is technically wrong. The result is mayhem for his opponent.

Naz and Brendan Ingle at the St Thomas' Boys Club Gym, Wincobank. One of the great partnerships in boxing.

found all day, and half the evening, shouting instructions to a wide range of different people, either in the gym, or in his own living-room, which invariably features a boxer making himself very much at home.

The gym has become a haven for anyone who cares to come off the rough streets of Wincobank. It is a tough school for those who have previously refused to be educated, and in Ingle, you have the headmaster. On any given day you are likely to find a complete cross-section of society, race, colour and creed, all sweating, panting and marching to Ingle's orders.

On one of my many visits to St Thomas' Boys Club, I spoke to champions, small boys, young girls, a physics student and a 56-year-old local millionaire, who is not allowed to fight professionally because of his age, but gets up to every trick in the book when he spars. And then there was a little, seven-year-old skinhead boy from just around the corner, the present-day embodiment of 'The Dead End Kids'. He may have looked like Tom Thumb when compared to the heavy-weight body of Johnny Nelson, but he is nevertheless brash, opinionated and full of depressing values. He voices racist observations in a thick, South Yorkshire accent. Naseem Hamed merely laughs, not at him, but with him, as he dodges the lad's punches in the ring. What does he, an Arab who suffered because of such preconceptions, think of loud-mouthed, racist kids like this little fellow?

'It's not his fault he's got these views and, believe me, by the time he leaves this gym, he'll be very different. You see, growing up as I've done in this gym, breaks all the barriers. Once they have been broken you can go back out on the streets and communicate with anyone.'

Ingle puts it another way. 'It's no use treating a kid like him softly. He's used to a hard way of life, so it's a lot better to start off calling him a little bastard. I've told him that if he doesn't like people from other races, instead of getting into fights with them on the streets, and then getting into trouble, he can come here and do it legally.'

'At least in here he's got a chance. You never know, he could develop into a champion himself. He's got real potential, and so much time on his side. And using our methods, he'll be safe.' He breaks off from talking. 'Come on, lad,' he shouts. 'Just think, soon we'll be in a big Rolls Royce and I'll be smoking fat cigars.' A huge, wide grin develops across the small boy's face.

As if to enhance his point Ingle brings a twelve-year-old boy over. 'Right then, Stuart,' he says. 'Tell us when you first came here.' The boy immediately owns up. 'Three years ago,' he replies. 'I had been expelled from school for bullying. I were a right tearaway. But all that's over now, since I've been coming here.'

For years the Amateur Boxing Association has frowned upon amateurs sharing training facilities with professionals, even though the practice is widespread, and their view has been as stern as ever when it concerns the Wincobank gym. This, however, is not an opinion shared by Sheffield University, who awarded Ingle an honorary degree in 1994 for his community service among the tearaways of the city.

The sight of boys fighting men, and the theory of providing a street education the hard way, may surprise the unknowing onlooker, but there is one more novelty to be found in this ramshackle gym. Ingle's use of gymnastics has, in recent years, split the boxing fraternity right down the middle, between those who appreciate the entertainment value, and the more orthodox who are appalled by such tomfoolery.

When Hamed somersaults and backflips his way to victory, most discerning viewers decide that this young man is truly an original. In many ways, of course, he is, but the source of his gymnastic displays can be found back at the St Thomas' Boys Club.

Ingle gathers three of his other protégés into the ring. At the trainer's command each in turn stands to attention, announces his

name and dives forward on to the canvas. The first manages a forward roll, the second completes a standing somersault, and the third produces a backflip. 'You've got to give them a show out there,' Ingle insists. 'I adhere to a particular theory – what they do is 99 per cent training, and one per cent inspiration.

But that one per cent is everything.'

It is through Ingle, and his unorthodox methods, in the centre of a depressed, racially-tense part of a northern city, and at a rather worse-for-wear former school hall, that the most gifted one per cent in the country learnt how to become a boxer.

The SORCERER'S apprentice

'Some kids come in here and don't come back', Brendan Ingle says, referring to the St Thomas' Boys Club gymnasium. 'That's okay. It's the ones who stay that really have it.' Nobody has stayed longer than the wiry Arab whom Ingle endearingly refers to as the 'Naz fella'.

While Salem Hamed's other two boys he introduced to Ingle hung around long enough to pick up basic self-defence skills before losing interest, young Naseem became immediately hooked on boxing, the gym and the Irishman who, he later admitted, became a second father to him. The feeling was mutual. Ingle felt, from the moment the seven-year-old first stepped into the elevated and solitary ring in the Wincobank gym, that he had a phenomenon on his hands. 'Only Naseem came every day without fail. Within six months this youngster is telling me he's going to be the best champion I've ever had – and at the time I had Herol Graham, Johnny Nelson and Brian Anderson, all champions, working in the gym.'

From that moment Ingle taught him everything he knew and Hamed, in return, became a hungry pupil, desperate to devour as much information and experience as he could about the fight game. Wherever Ingle went, Hamed followed, from championship

little, we just squeezed him in the back.'

His size posed a problem for the Ingle camp when he was due to make his boxing debut, aged eleven years old, at Sheffield's

When it all began. A young Naz goes to work.

fights to small-hall, six rounders, and each time the youngster listened, learned and soaked up the atmosphere. Even when he was not training, the boy sat around the gym watching his elders at work. 'He used to say: "Brendan, can I go to the fight?" He was so

Cutlers Hall. Hamed should have weighed at least 4st 10lb to fight, but was two pounds under. Unorthodox, as usual, Ingle stuffed lead weights down his young protégé's shorts and watched as young Hamed then proceeded to beat everyone in the Yorkshire

(opposite) Already dreaming. A young Naz listens, looks and learns.

With his hero. A victorious Herol 'Bomber' Graham with his arm around a young Naz, with Brendan Ingle looking on. Yet it was the boy who became the world champion.

championships. By all accounts, he impressed ringsiders with his stylish moves and hand and foot speed.

And so Hamed's education continued. Ingle took him to pit villages to fight older and bigger boys to build up his strength, continually inspiring him by pretending that Naz was fighting for the world title.

Even as a twelve-year-old, stories are abundant in Sheffield about the precocious Hamed. A former classmate, Nick Jones, recalled one incident at school. It was the final lesson on a Friday afternoon and, one by one, the kids shuffled uncomfortably to the front of the class to give a talk on their hobbies.

'I'll never forget when Naz was twelve and I told him that this fight was for the world championship belt,' Ingle recalls. 'If he won, he would receive £400,000, and I'd get a quarter of it. He went all quiet and thought about it. Then he piped up: "I don't know about that, Brendan. One hundred grand is a lot of money." The next thing, I'm in the gym and Naz comes up and says to me: "Brendan, I've talked about it with my Dad – you can have £100,000".'

Bored pupils yawned, or flicked elastic bands at each other, while their colleagues struggled to fill five minutes talking about scout camps or various items they collected. Next up was Naseem Hamed, who swaggered to the front, and nonchalantly flicked on his portable ghetto-blaster, filling the room with hip-hop music.

Without uttering a word, the tiny kid spent the next five minutes hammering the air with his fists in a cocky display of shadow boxing which left both the pupils and the teacher speechless. 'We had never seen anything like it', Jones said. 'We were all whispering to each other: "That was great." But we never let on to him. He already knew how good he was.'

At twelve Hamed won his first national schoolboy title, and went on to collect three schoolboy, two junior ABA and a National Boys' Club championship, as well as representing young England against young America, beating the highly-rated American junior champion, Danny Acevedo, in the process.

That night Hamed was the team captain – one of his best sporting memories – and he

The Wincobank gang. Herol Graham with, behind and to his right, the smallest boy in the gym called Naseem Hamed.

wore a gold dressing-gown. He vaulted the ropes before bewildering his American counterpart, who happened to be a junior Olympic champion.

Still the education went on. Ingle showed the lad what the game required – the dedication, the glory, and the pitfalls. He wanted him to see it all, especially the pitfalls. Ingle then began to include Hamed in the big Herol Graham and Johnny Nelson fight nights, letting him gain experience of title matches by giving him a walk-on part as an escort with his St Thomas' colleagues. It was Hamed who manned the dressing-room door after Graham's loss to Mike McCallum. And it was a distraught Hamed who paced up and down the corridors of a Marbella casino after Graham had been knocked out by Julian Jackson.

From a personal point of view, Hamed had no experience of failure. It soon became pretty clear to others that this young boy was destined for the top. If Ingle needed any confirmation it came when Mark Epton travelled from Mexborough to spar with the now sixteen-year-old Naz. Epton was preparing for a European title clash with Pat Clinton, but was given such a thorough beating that night behind closed doors in Sheffield that his spirit was broken and he never boxed again.

Hamed left school at sixteen with a couple of O levels and CSE passes, and got a job in a small telecommunications firm. His first pay packet was £63, and he soon knew enough to fit a new set of telephone sockets at his parents' home. Sheffield Telecom, under an apprentice engineer's sponsorship, allowed him all the time he required for training and matches.

It seemed to work in Hamed's favour. In an amateur career of 67 fights, he lost just six times, and even then Ingle insists, to this day, that on each occasion the young fighter was robbed. In any case, Hamed settled each score in later matches. The elder lads who used to bully the skinny little Arab boy had long since adopted a rather different view. 'Before they used to shout: "Paki, chocolate drop," and other things like that,' Hamed said at the time. 'But now they know I can fight, and they can see my picture in the newspapers, so they now all want to know me.'

By 1992 the trainer and young fighter faced a dilemma – should Hamed try and be selected for the Barcelona Olympics that summer, or turn professional that February, on his eighteenth birthday?

There was no contest as far as the ambitious Hamed was concerned. He was champing at the bit to start earning a living out of a sport which he was destined to dominate. Besides, Ingle was fearful that Hamed, despite his obvious credentials, might not even get the Olympic nod. Amateur Boxing Association officials did not approve of Hamed's showmanship and Ingle was convinced that politics would block Hamed's selection. 'Naz could have won the Olympic gold medal,' Ingle tells you. Instead, he turned professional and, Hamed being Hamed, even this usually run-of-the-mill event turned into an occasion.

So attractive a prospect was Hamed that he became the first boxer to launch his career at the House of Commons, and to be signed up by a sponsor before even throwing a punch. The Yemeni-Yorkshireman found himself invited by the Parliamentary all-party boxing group to the House of Commons. It

was here, in the grand committee room, that he signed a three-year British Boxing Board of Control professional contract, coupled with another contract for three years to appear on shows promoted by Barry Hearn, the London-based snooker turned boxing

Alan Meale, the MP for Mansfield, added: 'Naz is profound. Everybody who's seen him knows there's a lot of talent there.' He didn't say it, but you can bet your last dollar young Hamed was thinking something he has since said to various interviewers who

Business as usual. Another win, but Naz and Brendan Ingle have seen it all before.

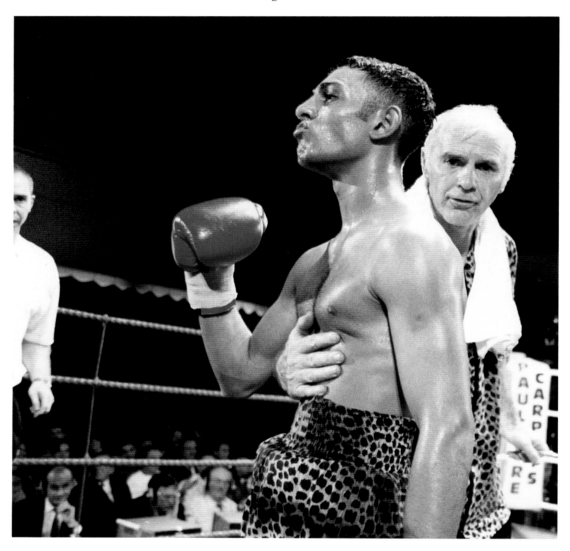

(opposite) No problem. Naz poses after defending his European Bantamweight title in Sheffield against Antonio Picardi, with father Sal applauding behind.

promoter. Joe Bloggs, the clothing manufacturer, also announced that they would sponsor him for what they termed 'a very, very good figure,' for this three-year period.

In welcoming Hamed, Frank Haynes, the MP for Ashfield, Nottinghamshire, and the chairman of the Parliamentary group said: 'This is the first time that anything like this has happened in the House of Commons. We are looking forward to you [Hamed] being the British champion and going further than that.'

tell him how good he is: 'So, tell me something I don't know.'

Two months later Naseem Hamed quit his job as a telephone engineer. From then on, he would be a full-time, professional boxer. It was what he had been made to do, and he needed no other source of income. Boxing would prove to provide more than enough. April 14th, 1992, was looming, and Naseem Hamed was about to go to work.

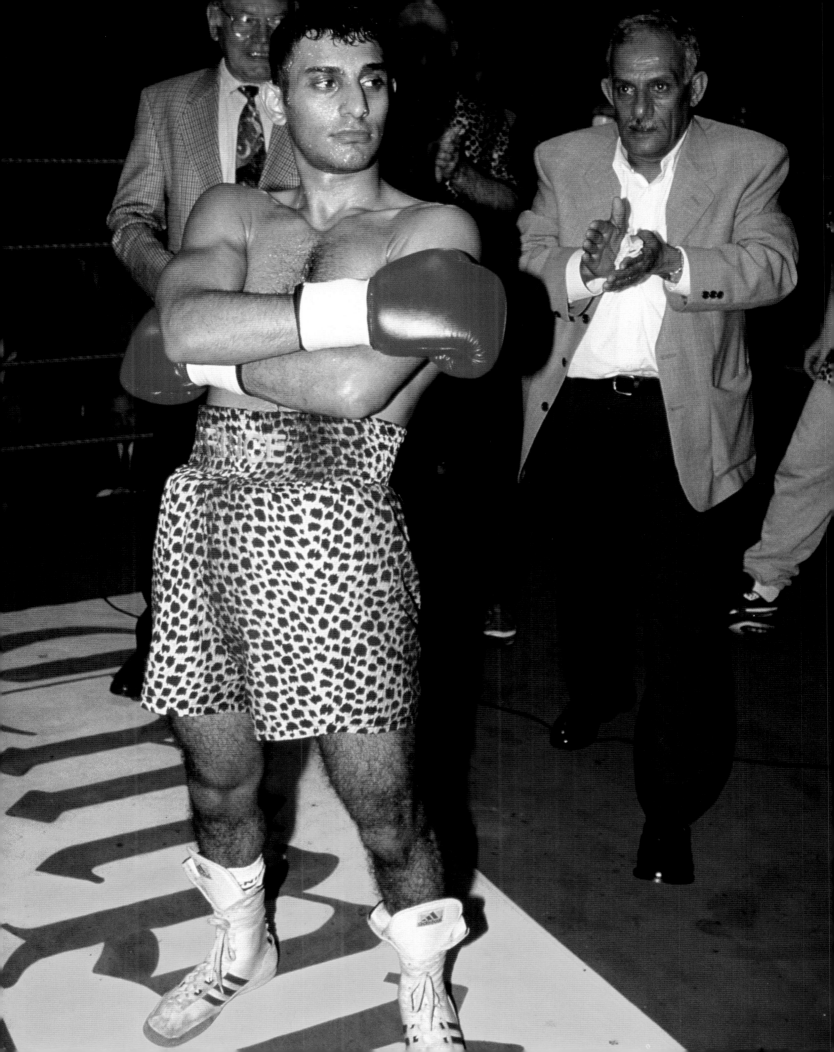

The PRINCE earns his spurs

It may be of little consolation to Ricky Beard, but he will remain forever in the record books as Naseem Hamed's first professional victim. The evening of April 14th, 1992. It was a fight that meant a lot to both men. For Beard, a seasoned professional from Hackney, he could hardly be seen losing to a skinny little rookie eleven years his junior. For Hamed, this was the moment he had been dreaming of ever since he had promised Brendan Ingle that he would become the finest champion at St Thomas' Boys Club.

Finding suitable opposition was pretty tough. Many felt at the time that taking on Beard so soon was a gamble. The Hackney boxer, who turned professional in 1989, and who fought under Barry Hearn's management, had produced some useful performances in his time. Beard lost against a future British champion, Robbie Regan, in 1990, only because of a cut eye in the final round, and again, to the British fourth-ranked flyweight, Francis Ampofo, merely on points.

Even Ingle admitted that, for a first-time

bout, they had ventured higher up in standard than normal. He added, though, that he was talking about Naseem Hamed, and Ricky Beard represented a first, tiny step towards a world title.

It was Tuesday night in Mansfield. Those who had bothered to attend the bill at the local sports centre were in for an unexpected treat from a young professional making his debut appearance. Hamed's purse that night, his first in boxing, was the princely sum of £600, and for that amount the youngster wanted to entertain his audience.

Vaulting into the ring in his leopard skin shorts, Hamed followed up a frenetic first round by crumpling Beard with a body shot towards the end of the next round. Revealing exceptional speed and movement, he had Beard in all sorts of trouble with lightning combinations throughout the second round, until the end mercifully came with 24 seconds remaining.

As his followers were to soon realize, it only needed one clean shot to finish the fight. Hamed celebrated with four somersaults and a dance of delight, before announcing, to an open-mouthed throng of local journalists and boxing hangers-on, that he had been quite prepared to let the fight last a couple more rounds, but had felt Beard needed to be punished. 'I wanted to put on a show for three or four rounds,' this still unknown, wiry kid explained. 'But I thought, what the hell: he was laughing at me behind his guard, so I let the body shot go. I knew he wouldn't get up.'

Beard remembers the occasion to this day. 'I was supposed to be one of the hardest-hitting flyweights in the country,' he recalled. 'I'd been fighting for fifteen years and he made me feel junior and inexperienced. He came straight at me and gave me a flash knockdown in the first. It was a combination, three punches to the chin; the speed and power did for me. Never before had I been nailed in the first. In the next round I stepped one way, about to throw a punch, but simultaneously, he stepped the other and threw one right up my thorax. I was really surprised by how hard it was. I reckon it would have put Frank Bruno down.'

The early days. John Miceli goes down in the first round in Mansfield.

An equally delighted Ingle breathed a sigh of relief. There had been so much hype, what with his own views about his little maestro, the Joe Bloggs deal and the trip to the House of Commons, that he was pleased to see Hamed clear the first hurdle in such emphatic style. 'He was a bit on edge in the first round and I had to tell him to calm down,' he admitted. 'It was a boy against a man in there, but the boy became a man in the second round.'

A mere eleven days later Hamed was back in action. This time the victim was Shaun Norman, the bill was Chris Eubank's world

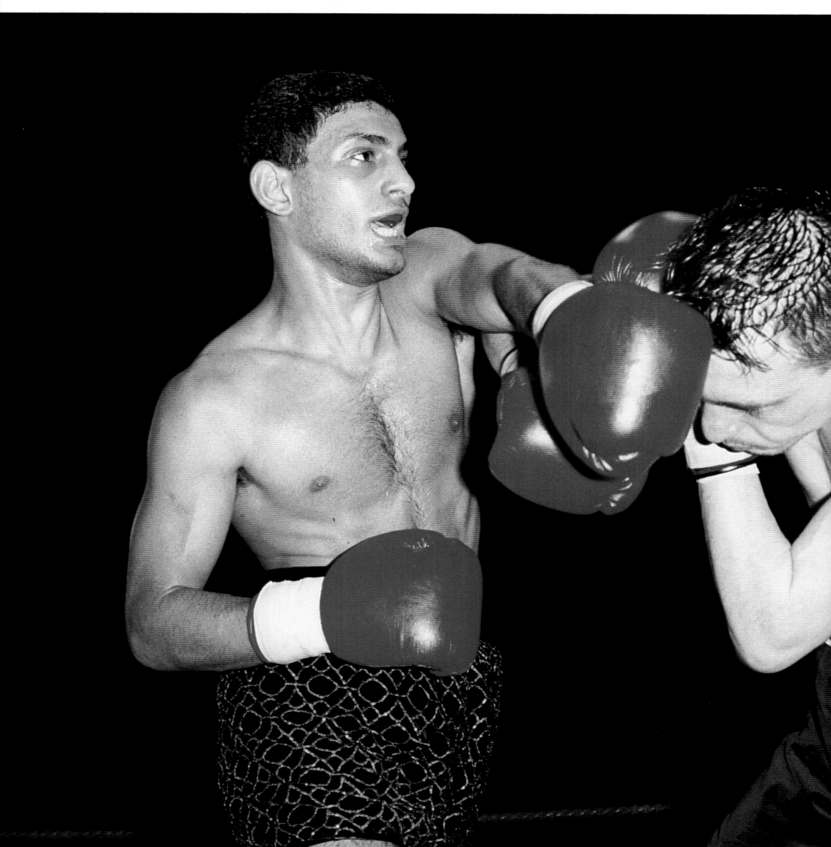

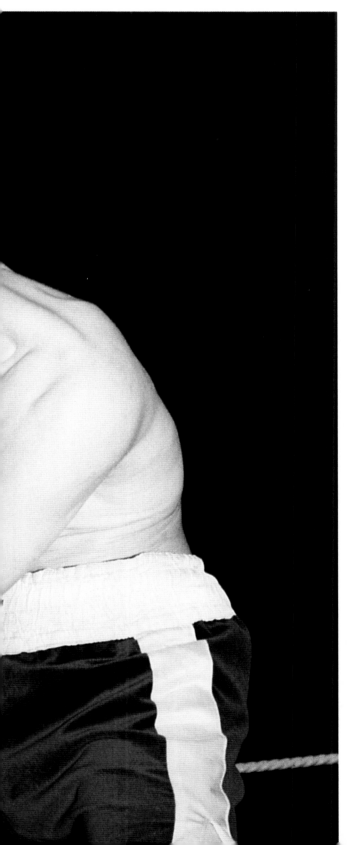

title defence against John Jarvis, and I was in the G-Mex audience in Manchester. It proved to be a similar story in the ring. Within a minute of the start it became obvious that Norman did not have a clue what was going on. He had never seen anything like what danced before him in his life, and neither had

I, nor most of the others gazing up towards the ring. The inevitable came midway through the second round when the referee had seen enough and stopped the fight. More somersaults and backflips followed, coupled with promises from an excitable but clearly talented youngster that there was much, much more to come.

Fight number three in Hamed's fledgling professional career took place on another big boxing night. Of course, Ingle had prepared his protégé for such pressure-filled occasions, although with Hamed's natural confidence, the big crowds and the television cameras probably served to increase his level of performance.

The main event at Birmingham's NEC centre that night was Nigel Benn defending his WBC Middleweight title against Sugar Boy Malinga, the South African boxer who, four years later, would finally relieve him of his championship belt. Four years ago Benn did enough to grind Malinga down to defeat. But once again, much of the talk centred on a seemingly inconsequential junior fight on the undercard.

Hamed's opponent was Andrew Bloomer, a stablemate and sparring partner to Robbie Regan, who enjoyed what should have been a huge weight advantage of seven pounds over the young man facing him. Instead, he went the same way as his two hapless pre-decessors. Despite the fact that Bloomer had never been stopped before, a heavy right hook sent him crashing to the canvas forcing the referee to end proceedings. Ingle did not even try to hide his excitement. 'Naz stole the show from Benn and Malinga,' he said. 'They were queuing for his autograph afterwards and Barry Hearn was delighted with his performance.'

After just three professional fights, Hamed had already made the news. In the latest *Boxing News* European ratings, for example, he entered the ratings at number ten, which was a remarkable feat on the evidence of less than eighteen minutes of boxing. Meanwhile, back at St Thomas'

One of only two men to ever last the distance against Naz, even if the fight was a little one-sided. Peter Buckley survived six rounds in Liverpool, in November 1992, but was made to pay in Cardiff, fourteen months later, when Naz stopped him in four.

moved up from outstanding amateur to the professional flyweight prospect of the year. The invitation made their wishes clear: the state wanted both Hamed and Ingle to pay them a visit, as guests of the nation. The plan was that they should meet the Yemeni boxing fraternity and put on a couple of exhibitions. Commitments back in the world of British boxing meant that Hamed had to put this offer on hold, but he was to pay his family's home country many visits later, all to amazing welcomes from an Arabic country starved of sporting success.

Closer to home, not everyone was enamoured of Mr Hamed. His flamboyant style, cartwheel demonstrations and general ring gimmicks were beginning to upset the Board. The word was that after Hamed dismissed Shaun Norman in Manchester, a Board official took him to one side to let him know what he and his colleagues in authority felt about the little showman. *Boxing News*, in contrast, were completely behind the new find, defending Hamed by arguing that the sport badly needed such a tonic.

Ingle explained to those who queried Hamed's showmanship what it was all about. 'You can no longer get by in boxing on pure skills, as Herol Graham will tell

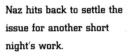

A rare attack from Alan Ley.

Naz hits back to settle the issue for another short night's work.

gym, an unexpected invitation arrived in the post, on official Yemeni government paper.

Word of young Hamed's startling progress had filtered back to his parents' homeland. The Yemenis had noted, with great pride, the manner in which Hamed had

you,' he said. 'The modern game, dominated by TV money, demands that something extra, especially if you are fighting out of a town like Sheffield, which has had to battle for survival for many years.'

His next three opponents all proved to be slightly tougher. Hamed made his first visit to a London ring as a professional to defeat Miguel Matthews on July 14th in Mayfair. By Hamed's standards, producing a technical knockout in the third round represented slow going, but I doubt that is any comfort to Matthews.

Des Gargano lasted one more round the following October, succumbing in the fourth to another technical knockout in front of a Sunderland crowd. Hamed put it down to

slight rustiness following the traditional summer break. That must have made Gargano feel a great deal better!

'He winded me several times, but it was in the fourth that he put me down with a body shot,' recalled Gargano. 'That last one doubled me up. I got up but still couldn't breathe after the ref stopped it. I've fought many, many fights, a lot against champions, and I take great pleasure in going the distance. Until I met Hamed, I thought I was indestructible.'

Then, in Liverpool, a month later, Hamed hinted that he might, after all, be human. Peter Buckley lost the fight by a mile, but at least he managed to survive the whole duration. After six rounds Buckley had

Naz's first appearance at Wembley, in February 1993. The unfortunate Alan Ley lasted two rounds.

Now it is Des Gargano's turn to feel the force of the Naz punch. He lasted four rounds in Sunderland when they met in October 1992.

somehow withstood Hamed's attacks, but at the time he felt disillusioned about the manner in which he had been totally out-fought. Buckley might feel a little happier about it right now when he looks at Hamed's unbeaten record, and discovers that he is still

history of the Boxing Writers' Club, the vote for Hamed was unanimous.

The new year started off with yet another connection with the Yemen, although this time it was a little nearer to home. Sheffield's Yemeni Community Association provided

one of just two men who have lasted the pace with the world champion.

Despite the 'disappointment' of winning his last fight of 1992 merely on points, the year was rounded off in successful style when Hamed was named the best young fighter of the year. For the first time in the 44-year

some funds on loan for Hamed in order to help him train and buy expensive boxing equipment. The Association's Management Committee spokesman, Dr Abdul Shaif, explained the reasons behind this support. 'Everybody loves Naseem in our community, and they all want to support him,' he said.

'We gave him our own money as community money. Our own members would do anything for Naseem because he is an inspiration to them. He is the only Yemeni to have ever made it in sport.' In return for the loans, Hamed agreed to pay everything received back with interest, and to allow the Association to sell fund-raising T-shirts bearing his name and picture.

Compared to his first year as a professional boxer Hamed's second, in 1993, proved to be relatively inactive. Word had quickly got around about this frightening new prospect, and there did not seem much point in facing him in the ring. Nevertheless, Hamed managed to find three opponents, who all ended their evenings inspecting the ceilings of the various venues.

First came Alan Ley in February at Wembley Arena. It may appear to be an innocuous fight in the greater sphere of Hamed's career, but the build-up was an event that remains in Ingle's mind.

The Irishman takes up the story. 'Naz was three pounds overweight with just two days to go before he faced Ley,' he recalled. 'That was a lot to shift in such a short amount of time, especially for a bantamweight. I told him: "This will show what you're made of outside the ring". '

'I didn't allow him to eat anything for the remainder of the Monday or on the Tuesday morning. Naz lost a pound during the drive down to London, but still had two extra pounds to lose. We spent a rough night, watching each other like hawks to make sure neither of us sneaked off for a drink. The following morning I took him for a walk, and by the time we got to the weigh-in, he was half a pound under the weight. He

A new approach from Gargano. If I stay down here, surely even Naz cannot hit me?

hadn't had anything to eat or drink for 36 hours. I took him to a restaurant after the weigh-in, but he couldn't finish his soup or his spaghetti because his stomach had shrunk. No matter, he still felt good. I told him that day that he'd grown in my estimation.'

In the second round, which had fast become Hamed's favourite, he produced a clean, knockout blow to end Ley's challenge. Returning to the Mansfield sports centre in May, the site of his first professional bout against Ricky Beard, Hamed then faced Kevin Jenkins, another seasoned pro. At least Jenkins lasted a round longer than Beard, and was saved from being completely knocked out, although the referee ended the night in the third round by recording a technical knockout.

His third and last bout of the year took Hamed overseas, for the first time, to Dublin in September. The Hull-based boxer, Chris Clarkson, despite his great experience, followed a similar route to his predecessors. Hamed delighted the Irish audience with a spellbinding performance that ended clinically, with a knockout in, once again, the second round.

By October 1993, Hamed had become big news, and a household name, back in the Yemen. In one of the more unusual developments in sport, the Yemeni government then decided to sponsor Hamed. The state education department started issuing exercise books with the boxer's picture on the front and back, that rapidly went into general circulation.

The Middle Eastern state also repeated its invitation to Hamed and Ingle, plus a party of eight others, including two sparring partners, to give exhibitions in five cities across the nation. Ingle had been sending over videos of Hamed's fights, which had then been screened on national television.

By now Hamed had caught the eye of promoter Frank Warren who, after the horrors of being shot, back in 1989, had hauled himself back from the brink of

personal and financial disaster to once again become the most dominant figure in British boxing. Hamed had turned his back on Barry Hearn and looked set to join up with rival promoter Mickey Duff, but when his friend, the Derby heavyweight Clifton Mitchell, joined the Warren stable, he soon followed.

Warren not only understood Hamed's obvious talent in the ring, but also his ability to put on a good show, coupled with his confident, charismatic persona. 'From the moment I met Hamed I liked him,' Warren recalls. 'I particularly liked his attitude. He wasn't shy in coming forward, knew exactly what he wanted and revealed a tremendous belief in himself. Normally, when you sign a new kid up, you have to be careful and patient, and slowly build him up. But this fellow was straining at the leash.'

In January 1994 Hamed had an old score to settle. Anyone would have thought that Peter Buckley had actually beaten Hamed in November 1992 instead of just lasting the full six rounds and still suffering a emphatic defeat. Nevertheless, to Hamed, a points win was a blemish on his otherwise amazing record. Buckley became the only fighter to date to meet Hamed twice in the Sheffield boxer's career. They faced each other again in Cardiff, and this time Hamed showed no mercy. The end came in the fourth round with a technical knockout and, for Hamed at least, the balance had been regained.

'Because I'd been the only one to go the distance with him, Hamed came out to take my head off,' said Buckley. 'He's so fast you just don't see the punches, and because he throws them from awkward angles you don't see where they're coming from.'

'And those tricks: he stares at your feet and when you look down he'll throw a punch. I wasn't fooled by that and tried a trick of my own by treading on his toes. He said: "I know that one", and then trod on mine and threw a shot at the same time. There's no-one like him.'

As if buoyed by his Buckley triumph, Hamed then recorded his most startling win

You're not thinking of getting up, are you Des? Gargano is trying to work out exactly what has hit him.

in his next, his eleventh, professional fight the following April. Returning once again to Mansfield, he laid out the unfortunate John Miceli before the end of the first round with a stunning hook. Miceli, a Belgian, was known to be a tricky and experienced opponent, who had never been knocked down before. What made the night even more significant was the fact that Hamed produced his one-round demolition job in front of ITV cameras. The television executives noted him with much interest, and quickly began to draw the conclusion that this young Arab may well be a bigger TV draw than Chris Eubank. Once Eubank had decamped to Sky Sports, ITV moved in to offer Hamed a highly lucrative contract.

It was all becoming ridiculously easy. Hamed grew and grew in confidence, telling all and sundry that they were looking at a future world champion who, by the age of 21, would become a millionaire.

The apprenticeship was clearly now over. It was high time the youngster was really put to the test. He had produced everything asked of him up to this point, but his next fight would determine whether Hamed was for real. A man like Hamed needed a title next to his name, and Warren and Ingle decided that it should be the European Bantamweight title.

The problem was that the current holder was an Italian called Vincenzo Belcastro, and there was no way he was going to give up his hard-earned belt without the sort of fight none of Hamed's other opponents had provided before. Make no mistake, Belcastro was vastly experienced, and widely respected. Now we were all going to see what Naseem Hamed was really made of.

BIG
time

Up until May 11th, 1994, there had been a surprising omission in the flawless and unbeaten record of Naseem Hamed. The Arab who told everyone how proud he was to have come from the city of Sheffield had never actually fought in front of a crowd in his home city. His meeting with Italy's Vincenzo Belcastro removed this small blip.

Belcastro, a recently qualified chartered accountant, was a veteran of over forty fights, including fourteen title bouts. He was a former world title challenger who had never been floored in his impressive career. Ingle knew that in Belcastro his little protégé faced a very tough man.

With this in mind Ingle, for the first time, took Hamed away for three weeks prior to the fight, staying at an unused room inside Rotherham United Football Club's Millmoor

stadium. Every evening they completed training by going for walks in the surrounding countryside. Hamed, in his confident and excitable way, was oblivious to what lay at stake. But Ingle knew. ITV had been seduced by the hype emanating from both Ingle and Frank Warren, and had taken the unusual steps of committing network dates for a product of relatively unproven ability. A win, and an exciting and convincing display by Hamed would catapult him into the big time.

The Ponds Forge Centre had been initially built to provide one of the facilities for the 1991 World Student Games. As you approach the city centre from the main road out to the M1 motorway, it stands proudly in front of you, a testament to the dogged way in which the city refused to be beaten following the decline of the nearby coal mining industry and, in particular, the steelworks. The night that the city's boy fought for the European title, the place was heaving with people, the majority of whom wanted some success after the ultimate disappointment of Herol Graham.

At the sound of a fanfare, the place erupted. 'Momma's Gonna Knock You Out,' a bass-heavy track, pounded out over the tannoy system as the diminutive fighter, with his sticky-out ears, suddenly emerged. If Hamed felt the pressure of the big night, he certainly did not show it. He and his corner men, led by Ingle, all approached the ring in leopard skin outfits, as if they were the Flintstones on tour. Everyone then expected to see the normal routine but, as a cheeky wind-up, the smiling Hamed climbed under the ropes instead. Impassive, Belcastro stared across the ring at the cocky little novice.

Within a couple of rounds the stare had changed to one of total bewilderment. Sure, the Italian was experienced, but he had never faced anything like this before in his whole

The first title. A confident Naz greets the partisan Sheffield crowd before his challenge for the European Bantamweight title against Italy's Vincenzo Belcastro.

The taunts that led to a muted press response to Naz's victory. Belcastro, a seasoned professional, is taken aback by his young opponent's cheek.

career. Hamed's main tactic was to rush in, at quicksilver speed, plant a couple of blows on Belcastro's chin, and then rush out again before his opponent could retaliate.

Using this method Hamed had Belcastro on the deck three times. It was an indication, bearing in mind how durable the Italian was, of Hamed's talent, but it also proved how tough Belcastro was because, unlike all but one of Hamed's previous opponents, he kept rising to his feet determined, at least, to see the battle through to its inevitable end.

By the tenth round Hamed was so far ahead, and the champion had been so confused by the amount of unorthodox blows coming from unorthodox angles, that he clearly had no idea how to counter the onslaught. He resorted to throwing forlorn punches in the air, while Hamed picked him off at will.

By the start of the twelfth, and last round, the contest was over. Belcastro, quite simply, needed to knock Hamed out if he were to retain his European title. As he found it

almost impossible to land any sort of punch on his slippery opponent, the chances of Belcastro succeeding were less than minute.

The fact that Hamed was required to fight all twelve rounds, far from inviting negative observations, merely enhanced his reputation as a boxer. We all knew about his skills, but what about his stamina and his patience? Now we had the answers.

At the end of the fight the judges' scorecards told the story. All three gave the verdict to Hamed, scoring the bout in his favour by 119-110, 120-107 and 120-109. Translated into rounds, these scores added up to Hamed victories by 10-1, 12-0 and 11-0. In other words, Hamed lost only one round on one of the judges' scoring, and absolutely none on the two scorecards.

Naz on his way to a convincing points win over an exhausted Belcastro.

Even this low down Belcastro is hit by Naz's unique style.

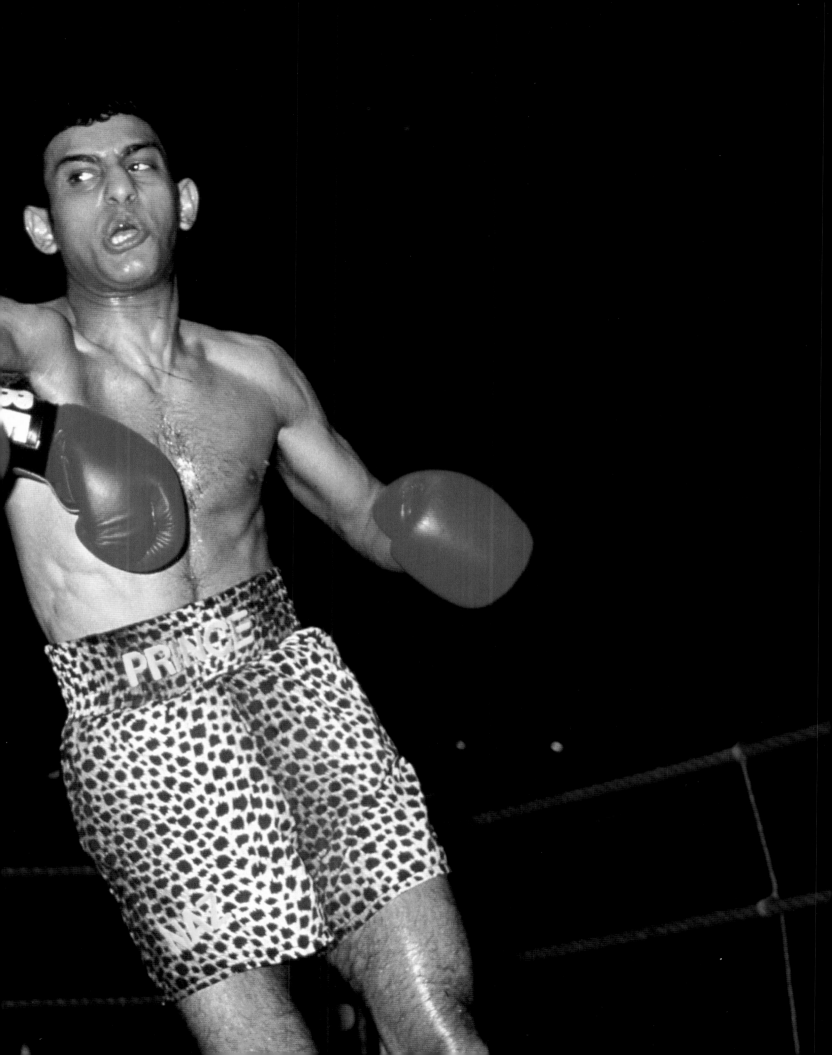

(previous pages) It's all
one-way traffic. Another
unorthodox stretch from
Naz, and a jab whipped
towards Belcastro's face
at lightning speed.

The beaten champion had, beforehand, been convinced that he would win. Understandably, when it was all over, and the Italian former European champion was back in his dressing-room, he was inconsolable. It was bad enough that he should lose his hard-earned championship belt to a twenty-year-old upstart, but what made matters a great deal worse was that he had no explanation for what had just happened out in the ring.

'Vincenzo does not understand what this Hamed was doing,' Belcastro's manager explained to the press later. 'He does not even know if Hamed understood what he was doing. He thinks Hamed is a good boxer, but he also thinks that Hamed should learn to box normally.'

The fact that Hamed had so convincingly taken the European title away from such an experienced champion should have filled the newspapers. Instead, it was the events during the last round that dominated the sports pages the following morning, and over the next couple of days.

All Hamed had to do to win was to stay on his feet. He achieved this, but also added a series of extravagant Muhammed Ali shuffles, jigged and danced around the ring with his hands up high in the air, taunted, teased and mocked Belcastro with his gloves on his hips, and even pretended to instigate nonchalant conversations with both Ingle and a TV cameraman. It appeared as if his self-discipline had been replaced with an uncontrollable urge to show off.

The backlash was immediate. Many, including Belcastro himself, were appalled by this seemingly public display of complete disrespect for an opponent in the ring. Hugh McIlvanney, the respected sports journalist, went much further, referring to the last round as a regrettable climax, and labelling Hamed as childish and insulting. ITV's commentators that night, Reg Gutteridge and Jim Watt, both registered their disgust at Belcastro's treatment, while John Morris, the British Boxing Board of Control's Secretary, also made his disapproval public. 'Nobody wants to risk killing the spirit of a youngster but there is no place for ridiculing opponents,' he said afterwards. 'In his own interests, he had better change his ways. The higher he goes in the game the more of a threat that nonsense will be to his own welfare.'

Ingle tried to explain his young fighter's actions to an indignant group of boxing writers later. He told them of how, during

Hamed's amateur days, Ingle used to make him believe that he was fighting, and beating, Sugar Ray Leonard or Roberto Duran. According to the flustered Irishman, when Hamed gestured to him in the middle of an exchange in the last round, he was being Leonard against Marvin Hagler during their contest in 1987. Ingle represented Angelo Dundee, the great trainer. 'That's what people didn't understand,' he insisted.

Meanwhile *Boxing Monthly*, the esteemed magazine, reported that it had never before received such a postbag of complaints about a performance, while the British tabloid newspapers immediately labelled Hamed 'Motormouth'.

A week later, I paid Hamed a visit back in Wincobank. Compared to most people, Hamed was still noisy and excitable, but compared to himself he seemed a little withdrawn, admitting that the torrent of criticism that hit him after what should had been his greatest triumph had hurt him.

'I was really surprised at the criticism,' he told me. 'I couldn't believe it when I read all the newspapers later. There's no way I'd ever go out and ridicule an opponent. I did it because everyone doubted whether a kid, who'd only fought twelve fights, and never gone six rounds, could last the pace against an experienced champion.'

'I wanted to prove that I was as fit in the last round as I was in the first, and cruising to victory, but I'll admit it's done me some damage. If I had my time again I still would have done it to prove my point, but nowhere near to the same extent. I'm still young and I've got plenty of time to change anybody's attitudes if they were put off by what they saw against Belcastro. Don't forget, I've had many people come up and congratulate me for not going over the top when I've been easily beating someone in the past.'

He pauses for a moment, before leaning forward, his face edging close to mine, to make his final point. 'I believe I'm the best boxer in Britain, and perhaps the finest to have come out of this country. In five years

time I will be a multi-millionaire and then I can let my family, who have struggled all their lives, live like royalty. I will do it my way.'

By his next fight, the defence of his newly-won European Bantamweight title, Hamed was back to his old self. People may not have forgotten his last-round antics against Belcastro, but they had largely forgiven him. The public, the media and the sport were beginning to believe what Hamed had been predicting all along. Here was a future world champion for all to see. Naseem Hamed had now found the route to the world title and he was eager to journey down its path.

(below and opposite) **The new European champion. Naz knows he has done enough to take Belcastro's crown.**

Defence of the
REALM

From the moment Hamed won the unanimous vote from the judges after the Belcastro hammering at Ponds Forge, every future fight would be both important and high profile. The Arab boy from Sheffield was a champion now, with a title to defend, and this meant that he, like Belcastro before him, had to defend what he had earned in the ring.

Of course, Hamed did not quite see it that way. Never mind defending his own title. That, after all, was a foregone conclusion. No, he was far more interested in collecting further titles, making himself a contender for a world title challenge as quickly as possible. So confident was Hamed of his ability by now, that if he had been offered a crack at the world title at any time, he would have taken it.

In the meantime, however, he had to put up with the slight inconvenience of defending his European Bantamweight title. Again, the venue was Sheffield, although this time the fight on August 17th was staged at the Hillsborough Leisure Centre, directly opposite the home of Sheffield Wednesday Football Club. His opponent was another Italian called Antonio Picardi, who had no idea that the man he was about to challenge, far from being nervous, spent much of the evening before the fight in my company.

Every other boxer I have known spends the day of a fight, let alone the hours leading up to it, with his own small entourage, and with his own thoughts. Not Mr Confidence, though. Hamed, lounging about his Sheffield hotel room, first spent a couple of hours in the early evening talking to me about the fight that night, and the way he first mentally and then physically outwits any boxer who fancies their chances against him.

'I only ever look into my opponent's eyes just before the start of a fight,' he explained. 'I can usually tell then if they're up for it. After that I just look at their feet. I remember one fight when the first words my beaten opponent said were to ask me why I kept staring at his feet. He spent the fight thinking

about that, instead of concentrating on beating me.'

I spent a couple of moments imagining how unnerving it must be to face someone

Antonio Picardi's defence is cut through at Sheffield. One hour earlier Naz was dancing in his dressing room.

who refuses to look at you when Hamed changed tack and started talking about his mother's extraordinary powers of prediction.

'I've told my friends that I'll win in three

(opposite) Naz moves round to Antonio Picardi's side before unleashing another bone-shuddering jab.

Four fights, but the same result. Armando Castro feels the force of a Naz left hook.

rounds tonight. What I haven't said is how I've reached this conclusion.' He paused, waiting for me to ask him to explain himself.

'Well, I always like to see my parents on the day of a fight. I've just returned from them now, with one of my Mum's special meals inside me. Sometimes she asks me which round I want to win in, and then she prays to Allah. She did it for my first two fights, and both times my wish for second round wins was granted. As for tonight's fight, I've just told my Mum I want to get it over with in the third. She went away and prayed, and then came back and told me it is done. So you see, my friend, I've already won the fight. The script's been written.' Poor Picardi. It's bad enough having to face a boxer with such breathtaking self-assurance, speed and skill, but to be taking on Allah

as well is asking too much of anyone!

I had to ask him why he was spending so much of his last, precious hours in my company when, by rights, he should have been preparing himself for what is always a potentially life-threatening, let alone career-threatening experience.

'Because all my work's been done, both in the gym, and in my head. I don't need to prepare anymore. Besides, I'm enjoying myself. I've dreamed of this since I was a small kid. I used to look at other champions and say that, one day, it would all happen to me, and more.' His eyes are, by now, welling up with ambition and, even more pertinently, total conviction. 'I see myself entering the history books, not just because I'll soon be the world champion, but because I'll be the first Arab to make it really big in boxing. I'll be a pioneer.'

He had spent the rest of the day sleeping, meticulously weighing himself on the electric scales in his hotel room, and paying the venue a visit 'to make sure everything is in my favour'.

Now he was ready. Inside his dressing-room, with his favourite 'jungle music' blasting out, Hamed virtually ignores the time-honoured, last-minute practice of shadow boxing, preferring to limber up by dancing in front of a wall of mirrors. His friends, from the St Thomas' Boys Club in Wincobank, including Johnny Nelson, are playing pool, shouting out the lyrics to the music in unison with Hamed. Ingle performs the ritual of bandaging Hamed's small but dangerous hands.

Then it is time. Picardi lands one good punch on Hamed, who refuses to bat an eyelid. Hamed, in return, lands countless telling blows on the Italian. Eight-and-a-half minutes of boxing later, and Hamed concludes his thirteenth straight win. I had chuckled at Hamed's outrageous story earlier that evening, but after seeing Picardi's fruitless challenge end in the third round, I thought again about Caria Hamed's prophecy.

As Hamed left the venue later that night he came over for a final word. 'You see, I told you, didn't I? I said the third round. So when

I used to look at other champions and say that, one day, it would all happen to me, and more.

I tell you I'll be world champion, and a multi-millionaire, you have to believe me.'

Two months later, a slightly heavier Hamed had the opportunity to claim another

Armando feels the full force of a left uppercut.

There must be an easier way for Armando Castro to make a living than this!

title. The WBC's Super-Bantamweight belt was vacant and the governing body decided that the two top challengers were Hamed and a durable and experienced boxer from the Dominican Republic called Freddy Cruz.

him which, in anyone's language, technically made him a novice. He was not supposed to be mauling seasoned and respected opponents. There seemed to be no reason to protect him from his own genius, but even

Never mind the European title, this next belt would help Hamed on his way to a world title challenge.

There were those who would, yet again, complain about the ease with which Hamed dispatched all challengers They inevitably raised question marks about the quality of his opponents. Yet the facts were that Hamed had only twelve professional fights behind

strong challengers, with impressive records, had no answer to the little Arab.

Cruz was yet another man with a reputation. In 56 previous fights he had never been stopped. Four months before he met Hamed, Cruz had only lost on points to Steve Robinson, Cardiff's World Boxing Organisation Featherweight world champion. Only two years before that he had lost a split

decision to the great Wilfredo Vasquez, for the World Boxing Association Super-Bantamweight title.

It cut no ice with Hamed. Two days before, during the pre-fight hype, Cruz had the temerity to call his opponent a child. On the night of October 12th, the child performed his now familiar process. It took less than thirty seconds for Hamed to show his power in a first round which saw him batter Cruz all around the ring. Hamed continued to dominate until, midway through the sixth round, a right uppercut seemed to knock all the fight out of Cruz, who was then saved from further humiliation and pain by the referee. Limping back to his corner, he gave one final, incredulous glance at Hamed before departing from the ring, his

Most boxers have known this feeling. Naz connects with a fearful swipe of his right hand, and Armando Castro's legs buckle. Moments later he will be flat on his back.

bruised and beaten-up face partly hidden by his silky gown. 'I have never experienced a man like Hamed,' Cruz said later. 'He would beat both Robinson and Vasquez.'

Now the countdown to a world title

Freddy Cruz is treated to a Naz right jab.

of defences of his latest title. Hamed only had eyes on a world title by now, but still had to make sure there were no slip ups in the meantime. After all, the men who challenged for his WBC International Super-

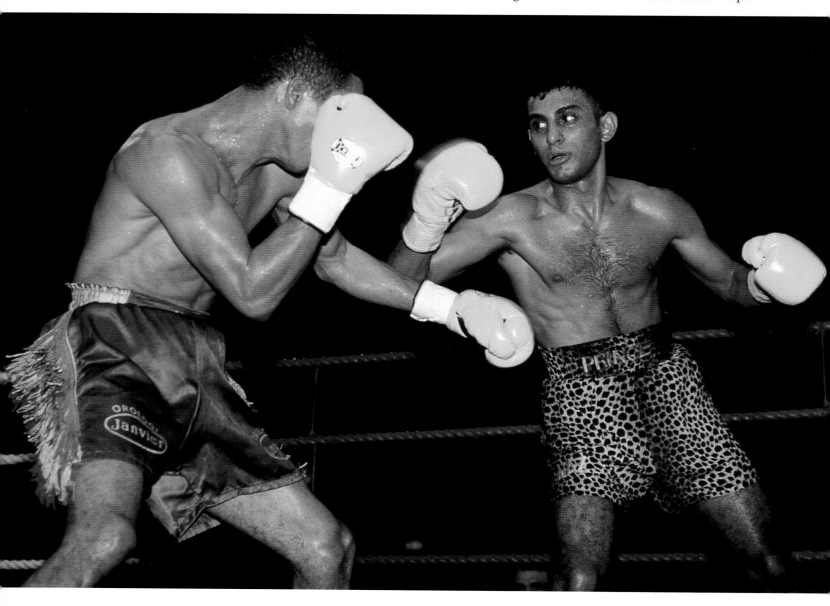

challenge had really begun. Frank Warren, having seen his man bamboozle another, supposedly top quality fighter, saw no point in adopting any other direction now than just straight up. 'One thing is for certain,' he said. 'He is not going to go sideways or backwards. Every fight will be meaningful.'

Once again, however, the regulations stipulated that he had to carry out a number

Bantamweight belt were all, in their own right, respected boxers. Or rather they were, until they met Hamed.

Another fighter from the Dominican Republic proved to be Hamed's next hurdle. Laureano Ramirez, ranked fourth in the world by the International Boxing Federation, had a good pedigree, but this was not enough to counter Hamed's natural talent when they met on November 19th, 1994.

In front of nearly 4,000 fans at the Ice Rink, Cardiff, Hamed required just three rounds to put to an end the eighteen-fight

thoughts in the following round, as he proceeded to take Ramirez apart.

Each time one of Hamed's largely unorthodox punches connected, the South American grimaced with pain. The grimaces

unbeaten run enjoyed by the Barcelona-based Ramirez. The fight began relatively slowly for Hamed, who seemed more cautious than usual, probing rather than rushing with his shots, and appearing slightly pensive. Some members of the crowd even showed their displeasure at Hamed's so-called slow start, but if they and Ramirez sensed a possible upset, Hamed put paid to such

became more frequent as the fight turned rapidly into a battering, and it soon became apparent that Ramirez had lost the stomach to fight the champion. Seconds before he was knocked down he appeared keen to walk back to his corner. Perhaps he should have done because, on returning to the centre of the ring, Hamed landed a perfect right hook which sent him crashing to the canvas.

Another classic Naz shot. Apart from the fact that he is totally off-balance, and fully exposing his face, this is a great shot. Only Naz can get away with such unorthodoxy.

There then followed a rare occurrence in boxing. Rising at the count of eight, Ramirez then muttered the words infamously used by Roberto Duran during his humiliating defeat by Sugar Ray Leonard. '*No más*' (No more), Ramirez announced, turning his back,

The champion was able to hit the challenger almost at will.

shaking his head and then walking to the comfort of his corner. 'I was hurt, I was dizzy,' he explained later. 'There was no reason to continue.'

durable and experienced fighter who, technically, should have been difficult to beat. Instead, Hamed dispatched victim number sixteen in four, pulsating rounds, confusing and frustrating the 32-year-old Mexican at every turn.

Scottish followers immediately took to Hamed, cheering him to the rafters at the Scottish Exhibition Centre in Glasgow. It was the kind of reception Barry McGuigan used to receive in his heyday, and it heartened many people in the sport to see, once again, a small man enjoying the popularity normally reserved for the heavyweights.

The signs were not encouraging for Castro even before the fight began. He did not stop complaining from the moment the referee, Mickey Vann, interrupted his pre-fight prayer. Although, for once, Hamed's first-round stoppage prediction was incorrect,

This time it is Laureano Ramirez's turn to be bamboozled by Naz's style. Note how Naz leaves himself fully open, with his legs seemingly off-balance. Yet, within a split-second, he is out of reach and safe, leaving his opponent swatting air.

(opposite) There's no way back from here. While Naz reminds the crowd who is boss, Laureano Ramirez lies flattened by the force of the champion's punches.

The defences would now come thick and fast. Each fight would be a hurdle for Hamed to clear if he wanted to reach that world title, and the pot of gold that would come with it. In Armando Castro he faced yet another

the champion was able to hit the challenger almost at will, barely receiving a blow in return. The end came in the fourth round. First Hamed put Castro down with a looping right-hander, prompting an outrageous

backflip to celebrate the moment. Then, once Castro had hauled himself back onto his feet, Hamed drove him back into a corner where the 20-year-old then unleashed a flurry of blows which forced the referee to issue a standing eight count. After a further unanswered set of combinations from Hamed, Mickey Vann had seen enough and stepped in to end the one-sided affair.

Later that evening Hamed earned the seal of approval from two distinguished 'small men' and former world champions. Barry McGuigan described the four-round demolition as 'awesome', while Walter McGowan, the world flyweight champion back in the mid-1960s, was equally impressed. 'This boy

at the Forum in Livingstone, for yet another defence of his WBC International Super-Bantamweight title. Once again his opponent, Sergio Liendo from Argentina, seemed to possess all the credentials. Surely the fact that the South American had never been stopped in his 50 professional fights said something about the standard of opposition facing Hamed.

It was a big week for boxing and the mood, both in the sell-out 3,500 crowd and in the ring, was a little quiet, following Gerald McClellan's sickening demise at the hands of Nigel Benn the previous weekend. For a few moments that seemed like hours, everyone at the ringside, and no doubt the

Sergio Liendo can't answer Naz's speed or reach.

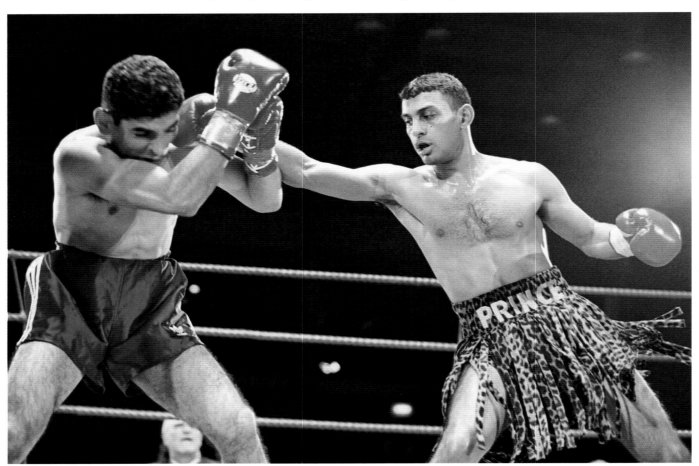

will win world titles in every weight he tries for,' he proclaimed. 'He is an exceptional, exciting talent.'

Six weeks later Hamed found himself back in Scotland, although this time appearing

millions of ITV viewers, feared that they had another boxing tragedy on their hands.

Out of respect for McClellan, Hamed deliberately toned down his showmanship before and during the fight. As Benn was a

Frank Warren stablemate, the previous week's events had been a little too close to home. When it came to his work, however, Hamed was in devastating form.

Shortly after the start of just the second round Hamed caught Liendo with a perfect left hook, followed almost instantly by a clubbing right. The Argentinean somehow clambered back onto his feet to receive the mandatory count of eight, but it was clear to everyone watching that, dazed and uncoordinated, he was in no state to continue.

To everyone's amazement, ever-mindful of McClellan, the Belgian referee, Daniel van De Wiele allowed Liendo to continue. The inevitable happened. Hamed hit the wobbly and defenceless Liendo with another left hook which laid him out flat on his back on the canvas. His head bounced up and down, and his eyes closed as he then lay, motionless and stricken.

Mercifully, after an agonizing wait, Liendo rose shakily to his feet. Hamed, clearly relieved to see his opponent had recovered, rushed over and cuddled Liendo warmly. 'I didn't want to hurt Liendo and he shouldn't have been allowed to take my final punch,' the champion said afterwards. 'I was so pleased to see him standing on his feet again I just had to go over to him and give him a really big hug.'

Later in the year Hamed was reminded of

Naz has seen it all before. While he implores Sergio Liendo to get up, his opponent studies the ceiling at Livingstone.

the Liendo fight after the tragic death of bantamweight James Murray, who died in hospital from brain damage following his defeat to Drew Docherty in Scotland. 'I've always known the risks and the dangers,' he reflected. 'The week after Gerald McClellan's horrific injury against Nigel Benn I was in the

The champion's pre-fight antics were, once again, far removed from the textbook. The night before, Hamed went to an all-night café with Brendan Ingle eating chicken and rice at 2 a.m. The next evening, on his way to the Shepton Mallet venue in the West Country, Hamed dropped in on a local

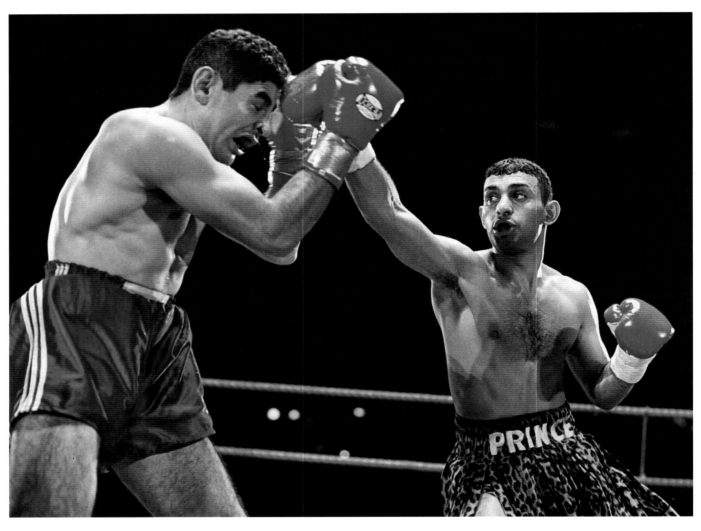

More punishment for Sergio Lindo.

ring myself. But nothing has happened to put me off my determination to succeed. You put a blank over what has happened and you carry yourself like a champion. I don't set out to hurt anybody. I just go out to win.'

This is exactly what he achieved against his next challenger, Enrique Angeles, from Mexico who, after thirty professional fights, had never known the experience of being stopped. Like his hapless predecessors, he had never met anyone like Hamed before.

bookmaker to find out what the odds were for an early knockout. When he discovered that a win inside three rounds was only 7–4, he decided against placing a bet.

Then, just ninety minutes before he was to somersault into the ring, Hamed sauntered into the press room and helped himself to a plate of sandwiches. 'I felt a little peckish,' he explained to the rest of us present. 'That little snack made me feel good and strong.' Yes, but Naz, what if you get hit in the belly?

His rather withering look was his reply. The interpretation was obvious – it just was not going to happen.

Sure enough, after just 55 seconds of the second round, Hamed retained his title by

the canvas. He made an attempt to stand again but was counted out on one knee by referee Larry O'Connell.

There was a certain familiar ring to the views of a stunned Angeles later. 'I was so

knocking out Angeles. A blur of punches at the end of the opening round knocked the stuffing out the Mexican challenger who had begun the bout with genuine venom. A fierce right hand, delivered while Hamed was moving backwards, left his opponent staggering, before a crunching left hook invited Angeles to become acquainted with

dizzy', he said. 'I have never been hit so hard.' Meanwhile Larry O'Connell, who had seen some of the world's greatest fighters from inside the ring, had his say. 'Of all the little men I have seen in a British ring, only Howard Winstone and Barry McGuigan would have lived with him.'

Hamed's problem was that he was too

Enrique Angeles and Naz share a second's glance at each other; Naz wins the psychological battle.

classy for his own good. It was clear that the various world champions had no intention of facing the little Arab in the ring, treating him as if he were the plague. Until Hamed could become the official, number one contender, he could not participate in a mandatory world title challenge. Instead, fighting as number three on the WBC list, he faced what turned out to be his last defence of his WBC International Super-Bantamweight belt.

His opponent was a Colombian called Juan Polo Perez, another veteran of 50 contests, a former IBF Super-Flyweight world champion, and a man who had fought nine world champions in his time. Defeats in his last three bouts suggested that Perez was in decline, although in his most recent reversal he had narrowly, and some felt

controversially, lost out to the formidable WBO Super-Bantamweight champion, Wilfredo Vasquez.

What made the night particularly significant was the venue. The Albert Hall had not seen a boxing match for nearly three years, nor a full house since the halcyon days of Frank Bruno and Charlie Magri, but on July 1st the old place was as good as full. If the fireworks display in the rafters was good before the fight, the fireworks in the ring proved equally as exciting.

Perez, making the same mistake as Freddy Cruz the year before, referred to Hamed as 'just a boy' before the fight. To his credit, he even caught the boy with what appeared to be a fierce right hook, following a couple of jabs, except that Hamed dismissed the punch

as if he were brushing a fly off his cheek.

Compared to his battered predecessors, Perez performed well in the first round, but if he had any high expectations, they were soon cut to pieces by Hamed, who noticeably stepped up a couple of gears, in the second round. The end was sudden. Hamed sent Perez to the floor with a resounding left uppercut. Although the Colombian rose to his feet after a count of eight, a flurry of punches, culminating in a glancing right sent the challenger back down to the floor, where he remained.

Hamed encouraged Perez to get up and fight, but his pleas fell on deaf ears. The Colombian had, after all, sustained a broken

The referee has seen enough and calls an end to the fight. A tired Enrique Angeles rests wearily on one knee, while Naz produces his customary cartwheel.

nose which, later, needed attention in hospital. The champion remained unrepentant. 'Perez said before the fight that he would rearrange my nose', he said. 'So I rearranged his.'

Watching in the audience that night was John Montano, the chairman of the WBO championship committee. Suitably impressed, he later gave his views to anyone who cared to listen. 'This kid has talent you can't teach,' he said. 'You have to be born with it. He has speed, skill, heart and a big punch. What more could you ask for? These qualities come together once in a lifetime.'

Montano had seen enough. So, for that matter, had everyone else. It was pointless holding Hamed back any further. Every time

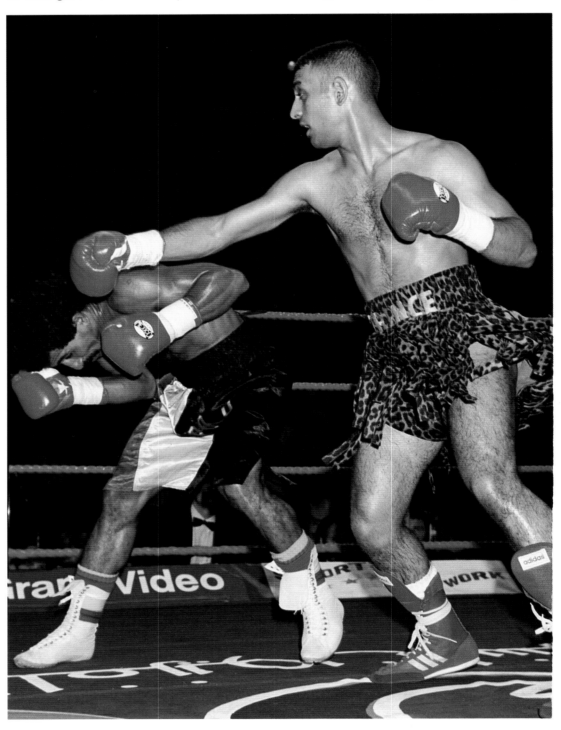

Juan Polo Perez can only look one way as Naz piles on the pressure in the Albert Hall.

a good quality, experienced, durable and respected fighter stood in the way of the youngster, they all ended up on the deck. He may still have only contested nineteen professional fights, but Hamed was clearly ready for a crack at a world title.

of pounds for this fight, enough to make Robinson, a man who had proved himself to be a worthy champion, believe that he would hold the upper hand.

This was the moment Naseem Hamed had dreamed of. At the age of seven, he had

Perez said before the fight that he would rearrange my nose. So I rearranged his.

The question was, who would be crazy enough to take him on? The answer turned out to be the Welshman, Steve Robinson, who held the WBO's World Featherweight title. Hamed would need to put on a couple

told Brendan Ingle that, one day, he would be a world champion. Now, at last, he had his chance. It would turn out to be an unbelievable fight.

Naz comes to the Albert Hall, but Juan Polo Perez is happy sitting on the canvas.

A STAR

is born

Naz can be a shy, retiring young man, as this entrance to a fight clearly shows.

(opposite) Naz sporting his new gold Rolex watch, courtesy of the President of the Yemen.

Nothing has changed at the St Thomas' Gym in Wincobank. The walls are still peeling, a sweaty smog still hovers and the surrounding streets remain largely poor. Inside, the scene is just the same. Part-time amateurs, kids, seniors and dreamers dance to Brendan Ingle's tune.

It is here that Naseem Hamed still trains, his feet planted back on terra firma by the familiarity of his second home, and his second father. Ingle is at his best, and happiest, when he is peering through the ropes of the solitary ring, barking out orders or lobbing pick-me-ups at his merry band of multicultural

Naz tries his hand at commentating during the Robinson v Domingo world title fight.

How many amateurs sign professional contracts at the House of Commons, and enjoy an immediate deal with high-profile sponsors before a punch is thrown in a professional ring?

What has always made a boxer in the past, though, has been television. Traditionally, this meant the BBC who, through the likes of promoters Mickey Duff, Mike Barratt and Harry Levene, screened all the big fights, from all the big venues, with all the big boxers who, in turn, became stars. ITV then jumped on board when Frank Warren bulldozed his way onto the scene. For all their outstanding sporting efforts, it was the power of television, coupled with the publicity emanating from the rest of the media, that made the likes of Barry McGuigan and Frank Bruno the major celebrities that they became.

The turning point for Hamed came in December 1993, when he agreed terms with Warren. The following April the promoter persuaded his old friend, Bob Burrows, ITV's then Head of Sport, to screen Hamed on a Saturday night. By this time Hamed was just 20 years old, and had only ten professional fights under his belt. The fight was against John Miceli in Mansfield and, with Hamed winning with a first-round knockout, the venture proved to be a tremendous success. Now a mass audience could watch a brilliant boxer in the ring, and a showman who, although not pleasing all of the purists, certainly entertained a demanding public.

Over the next twelve months a consistently large television audience saw Hamed bamboozle Vincenzo Belcastro on his way to taking the European Bantamweight crown, destroy Antonio Picardi, brush off Freddy Cruz in winning the WBC International Super-Bantamweight title, taking a million off the BBC's audience for an England football match once the first round began, and then dismiss Laureano Ramirez, Armando Castro and Sergio Liendo in ferocious style. By April 1995 Hamed, in television terms, meant a ratings winner.

fighters. Hamed, though, had dreamed of superstardom since the age of seven, and now he was close to it.

His amateur record, coupled with the praise from the plaudits, gave him an immediate head start in the star status department.

Hamed's rise to prominence, and his exceptional entertainment value, had not gone unnoticed in West London. Sky Sports had, after an initial rocky start, grown into major players in the increasingly competitive world of sports television. Armed with almost unlimited resources from Rupert Murdoch's News International Group, the network had systematically set about buying up as many major sporting events as possible. The catalyst was the Premiership soccer deal, when Sky's money smashed the myth that sport would always stick with the terrestrial channels because of the larger audiences. After that, the events all seemed to come Sky's way.

In March 1995, after a fourteen-year association with ITV, Frank Warren finalized a deal with Sky TV worth in the region of £50 million. For this, Sky could show every

Frank Warren promotion, and this meant Frank Bruno, on his way to finally winning a world title, and Naseem Hamed.

He was now still just 21 years old, but Hamed's financial future was secure. Win, lose or draw, the moment Hamed stepped into the ring to face Enrique Angeles at Shepton Mallet, he would become Britain's youngest boxing millionaire.

Back in the Yemen, Hamed had rapidly turned into just about the most famous person in the country, even though he lived in Sheffield. When, in 1995, he finally accepted their offer to perform in some exhibition matches, thousands of Yemenis turned out to watch. Even more lined the streets as Hamed made what looked like Presidential walks through the cities.

The President himself, Ali Abdullah Sala, had by now become not only a firm admirer,

Reach for the Sky. Naz becomes the latest big sport signing for Sky Sports.

Naz meets Rocky. Naz
takes it on the chin from
Sly Stallone at the Sky
Champions of Sport Night.

but a firm friend as well. He regularly telephones Hamed in Sheffield to check up on the young hero's progress. The further Hamed ventures into boxing history, the more his country, not exactly noted for its

devout Muslim. After he had beaten Belcastro he explained his values to me at the Wincobank gym. 'The way I've been brought up is different to any other top boxer in Britain,' he said. 'I've grown up as a Muslim.

sporting prowess, is placed on the map. Hamed had become a valuable marketing tool for the Yemen.

It helped that, despite his obvious love of fame, wealth and celebrity status, Hamed managed to maintain an ordered life as a

I've never tasted alcohol, and never will.'

'I've learned to live my life cleanly and to be a good person. When I become world champion, I won't let it go to my head like other boxers. And I won't succumb to the trappings of success. Although boxing's my life, I'm a practising Muslim and Allah is my number one priority. I haven't become European champion on my own. Allah's given me a gift and a blessing to go out and be the best boxer in the world. Before each fight I say a few lines from the Koran in the dressing-room. Boxing takes up so much

talent but they never had the discipline,' Ingle said. 'I've seen boxers throw their careers away. Naz, though, is clean-living. He doesn't smoke, he doesn't drink and he doesn't gamble. The hardest person to beat in the world is yourself, but to beat yourself you need self-discipline. Naz has got that

time but at the back end of my career I'll spend far more time practising my faith.'

It is all music, of course, to Brendan Ingle's ears. He has seen too many of his potential champions self-destruct. Tremendous, but ultimately wasted opportunities. 'I've had boxers before with great

singular determination to win.'

No wonder the President of Yemen is keen to promote his young friend. Hamed's face started appearing on boxes of tissues. Next came postage stamps. Then the personal gifts began to flow, starting with a gold, Rolex watch, direct from the President

World Champions, and both unbeatable. Snooker's version of Naz, Stephen Hendry, is visited by the boxer at the Crucible Theatre, Sheffield.

himself. Later, Hamed was presented with a £70,000 Mercedes, shipped specially from Germany, courtesy of Ali Abdullah Sala. Accepting the pink champagne saloon from the Yemeni ambassador in London, Hamed was clearly moved, particularly as members of his family were with him to mark this proud moment. Several times Hamed

lucrative offers. Glossy magazines, too, suddenly became interested in featuring Hamed's story, turning the lad into a model in the process.

Hamed bought a jeep and a Porsche. He then moved out of the family home, and into a mansion formerly owned by the famous soccer star, and soccer manager, Trevor

The awards keep on coming Naz's way. This time he collects the Remise Des Grants D'Or in Paris.

embraced his father, Salem, while his brothers, Riath and Nabil, glowed with pride alongside.

Hamed was turning into big business. 'We're building an empire around him,' brother Riath said. 'He doesn't have to work another day in his life.' Hamed found himself on the advertising hoardings, alongside the top-of-the-range Audi, with the slogan: 'They're both the most powerful in their class.' The Joe Bloggs clothing company struck another deal, while computer games companies, manufacturers of sunglasses and video producers were queuing up with

Francis. He started to wear Armani, from suits to sunglasses. All over the Middle East more than 100 million television viewers switched on every time he somersaulted into the ring.

Crucially, Hamed also started to become noticed in the United States. Don King, the electric-haired promoter, who has enjoyed, for many years, a stranglehold on the American, and therefore world boxing scene, had taken a great liking to the Arab boy from Sheffield.

He had first become aware of Hamed through his old friend, Frank Warren. The two had joined forces in the 1980s, just when Warren was emerging as a growing power on the British boxing scene. They struck up an instant understanding. King asked Warren to handle his European boxers and business and, when Oliver McCall beat Lennox Lewis for the Heavyweight World Championship belt, King was back in the big time after a

few years in the wilderness following the initial demise of Mike Tyson. It made little difference when Frank Bruno beat McCall, because Bruno was a Warren fighter. In turn, when Tyson destroyed Bruno, it merely confirmed that King, with Warren as his associate, held all the cards again.

Don King had watched Hamed's early

Naz reflects during training.

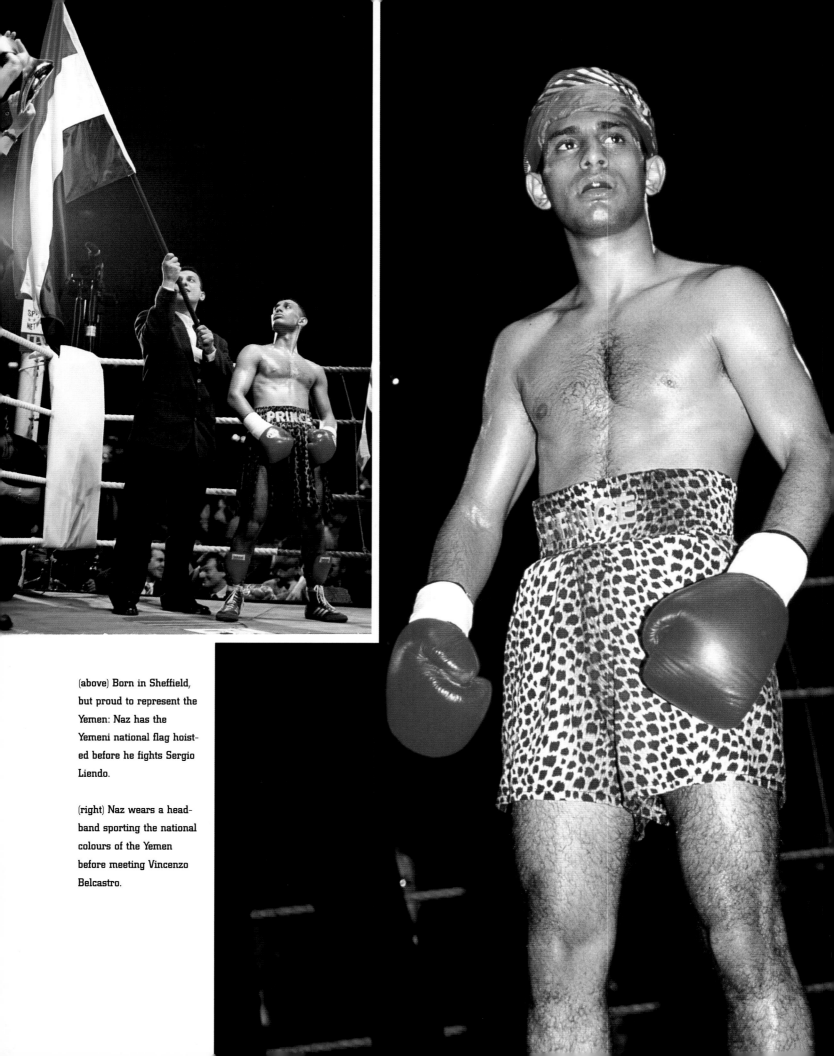

(above) Born in Sheffield, but proud to represent the Yemen: Naz has the Yemeni national flag hoisted before he fights Sergio Liendo.

(right) Naz wears a headband sporting the national colours of the Yemen before meeting Vincenzo Belcastro.

professional fights on the Nigel Benn and Chris Eubank undercards with great interest. He shared Warren's belief that in Hamed a superstar had been found. America soon sat up and noticed. Attempts were made to try and get Hamed onto the Bruno versus Tyson showdown in Las Vegas. It makes little difference. Hamed has already accompanied King and Warren to other fights, enjoying high-profile, ringside seats, and first-class, star quality treatment. *Ring Magazine*, the highly-respected American organ, voted Hamed the most outstanding prospect for 1995, while the likes of Sylvester Stallone, no stranger to boxing himself, of course, befriended the charismatic fighter. There were times during the 1995 Sky Sports Awards extravaganza when Stallone who had been invited over to London as a special guest, and Hamed, were inseparable.

Much to his evident glee, Hamed also cut a rap disc. Music may be one of the loves of his life, but it would be boxing, of course, that would continue to elevate Hamed's star status, and star earnings. Despite the temptations Hamed knew, back in September 1995, that he still had a lot of work to do in the ring. It would all mean nothing if his dreams of becoming a world champion were not realized. Now, after nineteen professional fights, only one man stood in Hamed's way. His name was Steve Robinson.

The fruits of his labours: a simple gift from the President of the Yemen.

on TOP of the WORLD

Naz's world: The WBO World Featherweight title belt sits proudly round his shoulder after his destruction of the former champion, Steve Robinson.

For a little over two years Steve Robinson had held the WBO's World Featherweight title. Many had previously seen him as nothing more than a good, journeyman boxer, but after surprising everyone and winning the world crown, he grew in stature. Some of the fighters who challenged him may have been hand-picked, but Robinson had also seen off the likes of former world champions Colin McMillan and Duke McKenzie, and was therefore well within his rights to hold his head up high as a world-class boxer of some experience.

On the face of it, Robinson would be enjoying two supposedly major advantages over Hamed. Although Hamed would have no difficulty reaching the 9st 1lb weight he sought to fight in the featherweight division, he had never actually fought at this weight before, whereas this had always been Robinson's natural weight. He was therefore, automatically, bigger and stronger than any of Hamed's previous opponents. Secondly, the fight would be in Cardiff, Robinson's home city, in front of a 15,000 Welsh crowd who, largely, would be screaming for their own man to triumph for the seventh time in front of them in two years.

Nevertheless, the messages coming out of Cardiff in the run up to the clash were decidedly downbeat. Robinson's trainer, Ronnie Rush, made his feelings public. Angry that the WBO had mandated the fight by imposing Hamed on his fighter as the number one challenger, Rush was at great pains to point out that this decision was made 'without Hamed even having fought as a featherweight'. He may have had a point, but it also indicated disquiet in the Cardiff camp about their own man's chances.

82

stinging blows, Hamed boxed from a distance and gradually broke down the Welshman's resistance.

In the fifth round Robinson cracked. A combination of blows dropped him to the floor, his first visit to the canvas for five years. Looking in bad shape he nevertheless rose to his feet and, using his gloves as a defence shield, managed to survive. The writing was now on the wall, and from the

There is universal disquiet at some of the antics Hamed got up to with Robinson.

fifth round onwards Hamed launched a fearful onslaught.

Like his predecessors, Robinson had never come across anyone, or anything, like Hamed. Despite the advantages of weight, experience and the crowd, it soon became evident that Robinson was out of his depth. As Hamed picked him off so his defence became shabbier. Soon any resemblance of a fight had gone. Robinson, a credit to his durability, merely took all the punches without response, as Hamed's fists rained in from every imaginable angle.

It clearly could not go on like this for too long. The fact that Robinson lasted until the eighth round was, in itself, a minor miracle. Then Hamed jabbed twice, switched to orthodox boxing and sent in a copy-book left hook that dropped Robinson onto one knee. Refusing to accept the inevitability of the

For a while Steve Robinson fought hard to defend his hard-won world title.

On September 30th, 1995 Hamed had to work much harder than before to use a wide range of punches to set his opponent up for the finish. Robinson, sticking to a crouch and a tight defence, was successful at first in drawing Hamed onto right counters, recognized to be the textbook response to southpaws. This survival plan seemed to be going well until, having taken a couple of

situation, he got up gamely but the referee, Ismael Fernandez, had seen enough and halted the proceedings. Even though Hamed, in producing his best performance in his

championship committee, was again present at the ringside. If he was impressed by Hamed's display against Juan Polo Perez in his previous fight, he was awestruck after

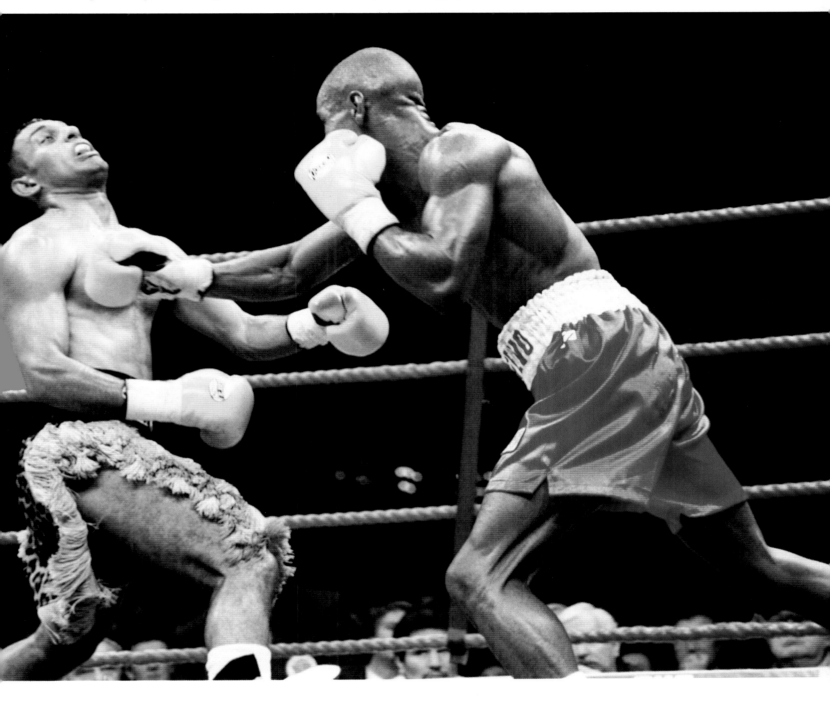

professional career, demolished the champion in eight, one-sided rounds, Robinson put up a good fight and at least tested the young pretender.

John Montano, the chairman of the WBO

seeing how Hamed had just dealt with the WBO's previous world champion.

'Naseem is fast going to become one of the best fighters in the world bar none,' he later said. 'He's an extraordinary fighter. He

Robinson even caught Naz with the sort of punch that would trouble other boxers.

can be as good as he wants to be, and he can go as far as he wants to.'

There was a chance that Hamed's crowning moment might, once again, be overshadowed by his controversial tactics. A

the Board's senior stewards, was quoted afterwards. 'There is universal disquiet among my fellow stewards at some of the antics Hamed got up to with Robinson,' he said. 'I certainly didn't like him waggling his

By the fourth round, however, Naz is beginning to take complete control.

few days later he found himself in hot water with the Board who criticized him for what they saw as the 'goading' of Robinson during the fight. Some observers found his clowning unacceptable, while others felt he had humiliated a champion who deserved respect. Lord Brooks of Tremorfa, one of

backside or the way he continually verbally taunted Robinson. I found it unacceptable. Hamed has so much talent and ability that there is no need for him to carry on like that.'

Hamed was genuinely surprised to hear this criticism. He had, after all, clearly showed his respect for Robinson as soon as the referee had ended the fight. Hamed immediately went over to the other side of the ring and extended his hand of friendship to the defeated champion and walked him around the ring. 'I predicted I'd win in four do,' he said. 'But I never humiliate a fighter. I try to break their concentration by being unorthodox, but that is not humiliating them. Muhammed Ali did it to all his opponents. If you break a fighter's concentration,

rounds,' he said. 'But I could not stop him. He was strong, and he took some great shots.'

On hearing about the disquiet over his methods from the Board, Hamed was unrepentant. 'If that's my style and that's the style to beat an opponent, that's what I have to

then you've won.'

His promoter immediately leapt to his defence. 'He did a job in the same way as Muhammed Ali did,' said Frank Warren. 'It was the same as Ali standing over Sonny Liston and saying: "Get up, you bum", and when giving Ernie Terrell a hiding and

A sharp uppercut to
Robinson's chin.

saying: "What's my name?" Nobody criticized him for that, did they?'

It all proved to be a storm in a teacup. Sky TV were delighted with the event, a vindicated Brendan Ingle, at long last, had a world champion, and Hamed had delivered what he had been promising for fifteen years. And still we waited for someone, anyone, to push the 22-year-old to the limit.

Back in the Yemen the whole country celebrated. Never mind the fact that Hamed lived in Sheffield, and had a broad, South Yorkshire accent. He was their boy, and he had delivered a world title to a country which, in recent years, through the ravages of war, had not enjoyed too much success. 'I am proud to have been born in Great Britain but I am an Arab,' Hamed explained. 'I am very

The proud champion is worn down by Naz's relentless punches.

proud to be an Arab. When I get into the ring I am fighting for two nations. In Yemen the whole country prays for me, so how can I lose?'

How, indeed, can he? A hand injury, sustained during training, resulted in Hamed's first defence of his newly-acquired title, against Mexican Arnulfo Castillo, being postponed. Initially expected to fight again in February 1996, Hamed's reappearance was delayed further by the slow recovery of

Now, he is gunning for all his rivals. He would be happy to meet the IBF Featherweight champion, Tommy Johnson, but also has Mexico's brilliant Super-Bantamweight champion, Marco Antonio Barrera, on his hit list. After that, Hamed is eyeing a showdown with the veteran WBC Super-Featherweight champion, Azumah Nelson. The law of averages says that one day, in the tradition of the fastest gun in the West, someone will come along and knock

When I get into the ring I am fighting for two nations. In Yemen the whole country prays for me, so how can I lose?

the injury. Any injury to the hand, the tradesman's tool in boxing, is a potential worry, and although Hamed continually dismissed suggestions that he might struggle in future fights, some talk within boxing circles continued to speculate about whether we had seen the best of the little Arab.

Said Lawal smashed this myth in 35 seconds in Glasgow on March 16th. The moment his head hit the canvas for the last time, Hamed's spectacular return was complete. If his right hand, the injured and therefore suspect one, was still damaged, then heaven help anyone who experiences a Hamed right-hander on full power. It was more than enough for the Nigerian, and for the few, red-faced doubters.

So, what now? Hamed plans to reach for the stars. He believes – and few will bet against him – that he can win four world titles, from bantamweight to super-featherweight. 'I want to set records. No-one in Britain will achieve what I can and will. I'm going to become a legend, as I've said all along.'

Hamed down. But first they have to hit him, and nobody has yet shown the kind of skill that will be needed to defeat the champion.

In the meantime, life goes on at St Thomas' Boys Club in Wincobank. Hamed may now be a superstar, but he is still part of the scene there. 'I can walk in there and there'll be loads of kids thinking: "I can do what he's done, a kid out of Wincobank, a kid out of Sheffield".' Perhaps, further afield, a whole army of Arab boys are thinking the same. Maybe, just maybe, Naseem Hamed will be the catalyst in a boxing revolution where, in ten years time, the traditional powers of America, the Latin American countries, and the Far Eastern nations, will be challenged by the Arab world.

Already there are some suggestions that another Arab will, in later years, take the boxing world by storm. His name is Ali Hamed, his trainer is Brendan Ingle, and his brother is called Naseem. Currently an eighteen-year-old bantamweight, he possesses great promise, prompting Ingle to talk of exciting times ahead.

(following pages) Naz knew he had the fight won by the seventh round, which is when the taunts began.

Naz admitted afterwards that Robinson had taken more from him than any other opponent, including this uppercut.

Now, though, and for the foreseeable future, is Naseem Hamed's time. At his age, and with his talent, Hamed looks likely to spearhead British boxing into the next century. Short term, his next step, apart from

as I grow older.' Better? Has anyone really considered the prospect of Naseem Hamed actually improving before? It is, to anyone considering facing him in the ring, a truly frightening prospect.

(opposite) The moment of triumph. Robinson sinks to the ground while Naz raises his arms in celebration. The Prince is about to be crowned King.

acquiring more world titles, will be to conquer America. Few 'small' men from outside the States have succeeded in doing this, but none have ever been like Hamed.

If anyone believes that he simply cannot continue winning his fights with such emphatic style, there is one more point to consider, an argument that Hamed, himself, readily accepts. 'I'm only 22 years old,' he will tell you. 'I can therefore only get better

A few hours after Hamed's successful first defence of his world crown, Frank Bruno's short reign as the WBC's Heavyweight champion came to a sorry end. Back in Glasgow, as dawn on Sunday morning broke, Hamed was disappointed to see his friend lose the title he had fought so hard, and for so long, to gain. But he also knew the significance of the moment. The artist formerly known as Prince had become a King.

FIGHT CARD

Prince Naseem Hamed
Featherweight
Super-Bantamweight

Five Time National Schoolboy Champion
Former England Schoolboy International
Twice Junior ABA Champion
Former Undefeated Bantamweight Champion of Europe
Former Undefeated WBC International Super-Bantamweight Champion
The WBO Featherweight Champion of the World

Sheffield   Southpaw   12 February 1974

1992

Apr 14	Ricky Beard	W	KO	2	Mansfield
Apr 25	Shaun Norman	W	TKO	2	Manchester
May 23	Andrew Bloomer	W	TKO	2	Birmingham
Jul 14	Miguel Matthews	W	TKO	3	Mayfair
Oct 7	Des Gargano	W	TKO	4	Sunderland
Nov 12	Peter Buckley	W	PTS	6	Liverpool

1993

Feb 24	Alan Ley	W	KO	2	Wembley
May 26	Kevin Jenkins	W	TKO	3	Mansfield
Sep 24	Chris Clarkson	W	KO	2	Dublin

1994

Jan 29	Peter Buckley	W	TKO	4	Cardiff
Apr 9	John Miceli	W	KO	1	Mansfield
May 11	Vincenzo Belcastro *(European Bantamweight Title Challenge)*	W	PTS	12	Sheffield
Aug 17	Antonio Picardi *(Defence of European Bantamweight Title)*	W	TKO	3	Sheffield
Oct 12	Freddy Cruz *(Vacant WBC International Super-Bantamweight Championship)*	W	TKO	6	Sheffield
Nov 9	Laureano Ramirez *(Defence of WBC International Super-Bantamweight Championship)*	W	TKO	3	Cardiff

1995

Jan 21	Armando Castro *(Defence of WBC International Super-Bantamweight Championship)*	W	TKO	4	Glasgow
Mar 4	Sergio Rafael Liendo *(Defence of WBC International Super-Bantamweight Championship)*	W	KO	2	Livingstone
May 6	Enrique Angeles *(Defence of WBC International Super-Bantamweight Championship)*	W	KO	2	Shepton Mallet
Jul 1	Juan Polo Perez *(Defence of WBC International Super-Bantamweight Championship)*	W	KO	2	Kensington
Sep 30	Steve Robinson *(Challenge for WBO World Featherweight Championship)*	W	TKO	8	Cardiff

1996

| Mar 16 | Said Lawal
(Defence of WBO World Featherweight Championship) | W | KO | 1 | Glasgow |
| Jun 8 | Daniel Alicea
(Defence of WBO World Featherweight Championship) | W | KO | 2 | Newcastle |

RECORD   **FIGHTS: 22**   **WON: 22**   **LOST: 0**   **KO's: 20**

THE TALE
OF THE TAPE

height: **5′3″**

fighting weight: **122 – 6 lb**

normal weight: **128 – 32 lb**

chest: **36″**

reach: **63″**

waist: **29″**

thigh: **29″**

fist: **10″**

First published in Great Britain in 1996 by
George Weidenfeld & Nicolson Ltd
The Orion Publishing Group
Orion House
5 Upper St Martin's Lane
London WC2H 9EA

A catalogue record for this book is available from the British Library.

ISBN 0 297 82173 3

Designed by Leigh Jones
Colour Reproduction by Pixel Colour Ltd. London
Printed and bound by Butler and Tanner, Frome and England